D1560148

THE POETRY
OF
E. A. ROBINSON

THE POETRY
OF
E. A. ROBINSON

Selected and with an

Introduction and Notes by

Robert Mezey

THE MODERN LIBRARY

NEW YORK

1999 Modern Library Edition

Copyright © 1999 by Robert Mezey

Grateful acknowledgment is made to Simon and Schuster, Inc., for permission to reprint "The Sheaves," "Karma," "As It Looked Then," "Why He Was There," "New England," "Reunion," and "A Christmas Sonnet" from *Collected Poems of Edwin Arlington Robinson* by E. A. Robinson. Copyright © 1925 by Edwin Arlington Robinson. Copyright renewed 1953 by Ruth Nivison and Barbara R. Holt; and "Introduction" by Robert Frost from *King Jaspar* by Edwin Arlington Robinson. Copyright © 1935 and copyright renewed 1963 by Macmillan Publishing Company. All material reprinted by permission of Simon and Schuster, Inc.

LIBRARY OF CONGRESS CATALOGING-IN-PUBLICATION DATA
Robinson, Edwin Arlington, 1869–1935.
[Poems. Selections]
The poetry of E.A. Robinson/selected and with an introduction and notes by Robert Mezey.
p. cm.
Includes index.
ISBN 0-679-60262-3
I. Mazey, Robert. II. Title.
PS3535.O25A6 1999
811'.52—dc21 98-31800

Modern Library website address: www.modernlibrary.com

Printed in the United States of America on acid-free paper

2 4 6 8 9 7 5 3 1

For John Hollander and Natalie Charkow

ACKNOWLEDGMENTS

I am greatly indebted to a number of people, living and dead. My first thanks must go to Denham Sutcliffe, whose eloquent passion for American literature and for Robinson in particular made his classroom an occasion of pleasure and excitement not to be missed; I am also grateful for *Untriangulated Stars,* his edition of Robinson's most interesting letters, those to Harry DeForest Smith. My classmate James Wright taught me Robinson in his own way, which was to transfix us, his friends and rapt auditors, with some of the many Robinson poems he had by heart; that was my first encounter with "The Wandering Jew," "Veteran Sirens," and "Isaac and Archibald." All this was heady stuff for the boy I was then, and it has remained fresh in my memory for nearly fifty years. The conversations I have had at one time or another with Donald Justice and Alan Trachtenberg and John Hollander have been illuminating, and I kept in mind their good advice and suggestions while deciding on my selection of poems for this volume. John Hollander was an unfailing resource whenever I found myself puzzled or stymied in composing my notes; and I was also supplied with some useful information by John

Stauffer, and by Mark Melnicove, Joanne D. Clark, and Danny Smith of Gardiner, Maine. Danny Smith, who may know more about Gardiner and Robinson's life there than anyone else alive, was unstinting with his knowledge and generous with some unpublished material that I have quoted from in my notes. (He also tactfully corrected my errors.) I have been fortunate in my learned and sympathetic colleagues, of whom Dick Barnes and Howard Young were especially helpful. Donald Justice, Alan Trachtenberg, Norman Fruman, Thomas Pinney, Naomi Mezey, Dick Barnes, and others kindly read the manuscript of my introductory essay or of my notes, or both, and proposed a number of unquestionable improvements. I thank the editors of *The New Criterion,* in which "Laïs Dedicates to Aphroditê the Tools of Her Trade" first appeared. And I thank Jessica Roberts and William Spengemann for introducing me to the poems of Sarah Morgan Piatt. I appreciate the hours that Jodie Hollander and Greg Hauser worked to establish a reasonably correct text. Without the expert and diligent help of Gerald Laffoon of the Pomona College Academic Computing Center, this book would have been delayed God knows how long. I am indebted to a number of books: *Edwin Arlington Robinson,* by Yvor Winters; *Edwin Arlington Robinson: The Life of Poetry,* by Louis Coxe; *Next Door to a Poet,* by Rollo Walter Brown; *Edwin Arlington Robinson: The Literary Background of a Traditional Poet,* by Edwin S. Fussell; and *Uncollected Poems and Prose by Edwin Arlington Robinson,* an invaluable book edited by Richard Cary. Whatever their shortcomings, Hermann Hagedorn's biography, *Edwin Arlington Robinson,* and Chard Powers Smith's, *Where the Light Falls,* have been indispensable. I have made use of some excellent short works: essays by Irving Howe, Morton Dauwen Zabel, and J. V. Cunningham; Robert Frost's beautiful introduction to *King Jasper;* Donald Justice's preface to Mark Melnicove's facsimile reprinting of *The Torrent and the Night Before* (as well as his essay "Benign Obscurity," which can be found in his recent collection of prose, *Oblivion*); James Dickey's introduction to Morton Dauwen Zabel's edition of Robinson's selected poems; and Donald Hall's introduction to *The Essential Robinson*. And to conclude, I thank my editor, Ian Jackman, for his patience and forbearance and for his criticism and suggestions.

Contents

INTRODUCTION

I

No one yet has been able to give a wholly accurate account of Edwin Arlington Robinson's life, or convey a persuasively vivid sense of the sort of man he was; it may not be possible. Of all the poets the reality of whose lives I have tried to imagine, he is perhaps the most elusive, the most shadowy. In comparison, the tenaciously private Hardy seems almost an open book. J. V. Cunningham has written, "Robinson was a man almost without biography who became a legend to his friends. . . . He knew we do not really know about others; we do not know about him." We know about him largely through his poems, which is surely how he would have wished it to be.

Robinson was born on December 22, 1869 in Head Tide, a tiny Maine village near the coast. He was the youngest of three sons, his brother Herman five years older and Dean more than twelve. His mother, Mary Elizabeth née Palmer, was descended from Thomas Dudley, second governor of the Massachusetts Bay Colony, one of whose daughters was Anne Bradstreet, "the Tenth Muse Lately Sprung up in America." His father, Edward, who came from a long line of carpenters and shipwrights, grew up in straitened circumstances. After a few years as a schoolteacher, he began speculating in standing timber and made a great deal of money, which he invested in profitable mortgages. During Robinson's first year, the family moved into a large, comfortable house in nearby Gardiner, a bustling town of nearly five thousand on the banks of the Kennebec River, prosperous with pulp, paper, and lumber mills, and ice cutting and shipping. (Ice cut from the Kennebec in winter was shipped all over the world—some of it cooled the drinks of British officers in India.) There Edward kept a store, loaned money, sat on the boards of banks, and eventually served in the state legislature.

Edwin Arlington seems a stately enough name, but Robinson hated it. That no doubt had something to do with the way he got it. Having already had two sons, his parents, especially his mother, had their hearts set on a girl; a third son was such a disappointment that they neglected to name him for many months. While the Robinsons were vacationing at the coastal resort of Harpswell during the summer of 1870, one of the guests at a lawn party urged that the child be given a name, which was then picked out of a hat. The woman who had jotted down the "winning" name was a native of Arlington, Massachusetts—that settled the question of a middle name. (I have sometimes wondered if that nonchalant and offhand christening was not the source of Robinson's penchant for assigning so many of his characters arbitrary, peculiar, often outlandish names—Tasker Norcross, for example, or Bewick Finzer, Roman Bartholow, Umfraville, Miniver Cheevy, Sainte-Nitouche, to list but a few.)

We know little about his boyhood, which seems to have been for the most part uneventful and not unhappy. He went to school, skated on the Kennebec in winter, wandered around Gardiner, fished, read books, and worked around the house— splitting and piling wood, looking after the vegetable garden. He would certainly have been aware that his brother Dean was his father's favorite, and his brother Herman his mother's; Win, as he was then called, was, as he would be all his life, the odd man out. I do not mean to say that he was abused or unloved; but he loved them more than they loved him, and they were as unaware of his great gift as almost everyone else in Gardiner. He felt special very early—not superior, just different, an outsider even in his own family. That loneliness and sense of separation were soon intertwined with what he began to recognize as his vocation. It was inescapably his fate: he had been called, and he had been chosen. Although shy and inward and not a particularly good student, he was an avid and acquisitive reader, and by the age of eleven already intensely interested in poetry. Despite his taciturn nature and social awkwardness, he had a gift for friendship; he and two or three intimates liked to gather in a little-used room in the high school to smoke, drink toddies, talk about girls, and read poetry aloud. (On one occasion, after his friends had shown little enthusiasm for a batch of his poems, he threw them into the stove, so destroying nearly all his juvenilia.)

There were two important events in his boyhood that must be mentioned. When he was eleven or twelve, a teacher boxed him on the ear, because, it is said, he had been daydreaming. I am a little skeptical of the origin of that story some hundred and twenty years later; but be that as it may, it was a serious blow. The eardrum and mastoid bone were damaged, and the chronic injury not only caused some loss of hearing but flared up periodically into infections and bouts of pain, sometimes very severe pain, that would trouble him to the end of his life. On one occasion it was, as we shall see, a piece of luck.

The other and equally fateful event was his encounter, at age fifteen, with Dr. Alanson Tucker Schumann, a homœopathic physician who had given up his medical practice to satisfy a passion for poetry, especially for sonnets and the more intricate French forms. Several writers have spoken of Schu-

mann as a poetaster, but that is unjust. I have read several of
his sonnets, and I think that Yvor Winters was accurate when
he said of one of them, "This is not immortal poetry, but in
spite of a few trite phrases it has a kind of plain honesty which
is not unlike the plain honesty of much of the best of Robin-
son. Schumann must have been a man of some intelligence,
and it is possible that he may have had an influence on the for-
mation of Robinson's style." What is remarkable is that Dr.
Schumann recognized the young man's talent immediately
and was unselfish and perceptive enough to realize that it was
greater than his own. He took young Robinson under his wing
and introduced him to his poetry circle, a small group of pas-
sionate amateurs who were also deeply involved with the dif-
ficult forms like the villanelle and the ballade. This work must
have quickly improved his grasp of technique and his metri-
cal practice. Louis Coxe said, "If we may be permitted a pa-
tronizing smile at what that society was like, it took Robinson
in when he was a mere boy and it did not patronize him." And
J. V. Cunningham has written that meter is "a language which,
like any language, must be learned young or never. And as a
language it must have an audience; this the doctor and a cul-
tivated local poetic circle provided, so that in his later career
he never faltered in meter, and at his most involved and ob-
scure is still speaking to an audience."

Of all the sorrows and ordeals that the next ten years were
to bring, the first and perhaps most painful was the sudden
breakdown of his brother Dean, whom he loved and admired,
and of whom he would say many years later, "Dean knew
more at twenty than I shall ever know." After graduating from
Bowdoin, Dean had hoped to devote himself to medical re-
search, but his father, always the hardheaded Yankee, insisted
on his opening a practice. The life of a country doctor was
very demanding, particularly in winter; and Dean, often rid-
ing a horse or rowing a boat on bitter nights to visit his pa-

tients, suffered from unbearable neuralgic pain, which he tried to ease with alcohol and morphine. The dangers of morphine were not then so well known as now, and it was not uncommon for doctors to abuse it unwittingly. Then, compounding his misery, he lost his fiancée. There is no further information about this; she disappears from the record of these years, and we are left to suppose that she broke off their engagement. In 1888, before Win had finished high school, Dean was back in the house in Gardiner for good, incurably addicted.

Sometime that year, Edwin and Herman met Emma Shepherd, whose family had recently moved to Gardiner, and both fell in love with her. As one can see from photographs, she was extraordinarily beautiful. It has been said that Dean too was attracted to her, and there were others, but in Win's mind, it came down to Herman and himself. Insofar as there was really any competition, he was at a distinct disadvantage. He was just finishing high school; Emma was in her early twenties, close to Herman's age. Win tended to be tongue-tied, especially in the presence of women, and he probably had not the slightest idea of how to go about courting one—it is unlikely that he even thought to propose. Being so deeply in love, believing her to be his soul mate, he may well have imagined that her feelings were, had to be, the same. No doubt she liked him, and admired his literary gifts, but she could not have taken him seriously as a suitor. It was obvious by then to everyone who knew him that he was, for better or worse, married to poetry; he had no trade, no practical ability, no interest in earning a living, let alone supporting a wife and family. It was no contest: Herman was everything that he was not—athletic, voluble and outgoing, handsome and quick-witted, and, above all, a go-getter. He was already a promising young employee in a Gardiner bank, impressing his superiors with his boundless self-confidence and ambition.

That Edwin loved his brother there is little question, but

he also regarded Herman with a mixture of envy and contempt—not only as the loved son and the triumphant suitor but as a young man to be reckoned with, on his way to brilliant success in the "real" world of competition for goods and status—the world that Robinson despised. And Herman's winning Emma's hand kindled in him the pain and anger that can be seen all too clearly in the poem "Cortège," written shortly after their marriage two years later.

After finishing high school, Robinson would live at home for most of the next ten years. He would dearly have loved to go on to college, but his father, despite his own youthful stint as a schoolteacher, had no use for colleges, and the wreckage of Dean's life could only have hardened his conviction of the worthlessness of book learning.

Robinson had neither need nor desire to look for a job—as far as he was concerned, he *had* a job: he was a poet. He was not at all lazy—he did more than his share of the necessary chores inside the house and outside; and he was hard at work learning his craft, reading and writing incessantly. He translated one of Cicero's orations into blank verse; he translated Horace's ode I, 11 (later to be revised into the lovely "Horace to Leuconoë"); and perhaps most fruitful for his development, he was translating Virgil, who, like Shakespeare, was one of his masters—and with considerable skill for a young man barely twenty. A few lines from his version of the galley race from Book V of *The Aeneid:*

> ... from the fateful rock released, Sergestus
> Paddled with scanty oars his crippled craft,
> Scoffed and unhonored. As a snake, o'ertaken
> Upon the highway, which a wheel has crossed
> Or traveller with heavy blow has struck
> And left half-dead and ground beneath a rock,
> Vainly retreating, curls its tortuous length

And hissing rears its head with glittering eyes,
Ferocious; though retarded by the wound
Twisting and writhing struggles on its way,
So the slow ship worked inward to the shore.

He was reading and rereading Shakespeare and Milton; although disliking the excesses of Blake and Shelley, he loved Keats and Wordsworth; Cowper was important to him, and Crabbe; so were Browning and Kipling. Hoyt H. Hudson, Richard Wilbur, and others have noticed his debt to W. M. Praed, the early nineteenth-century master of *vers de société*. Most critics have assumed that he was chiefly influenced by the English poets, but Edwin Fussell has shown clearly how carefully and lovingly he read Longfellow, Emerson, and Thoreau, and how closely "Isaac and Archibald" was modeled on Bryant's "The Old Man's Counsel." And I suspect that the long-neglected and underrated Sarah Morgan Piatt—one of the very few late nineteenth-century poets in America to write, at least sometimes, in a natural language that approximates real speech—may have influenced him, or at least reinforced his disposition toward the plain style and his taste for the colloquial. But as Louis Coxe wrote, Robinson is a poet "with a prose in view," who was formed as much if not more by novelists as by poets, especially Hawthorne and, later, Henry James; during these years he was also passionately reading Daudet, Zola, Flaubert, Meredith, and Hardy. And of course, always, the King James Bible.

In 1890, Herman and Emma were married—Edwin did not attend the wedding—and left for St. Louis, where they would spend their honeymoon and where Herman would resume his business dealings. He was already well known there and marked by the local papers as a young man on the rise. By this time, his father had handed over to him the management of almost all of the family fortune, which Herman was busily investing, along with the funds of other Maine businessmen, in land in Kansas, Missouri, and Minnesota. However much anguish the marriage had caused him, Win must have felt some relief that the sources of that anguish were for the moment far away.

By the time the couple returned the following year, Edwin's ear trouble had flared up again; he was in terrible pain, and it was imperative that he go to Boston to be under the care of a specialist. Herman, in an act more generous than he could know, proposed that, inasmuch as Edwin would have to stay in Boston for some months in any case, and the family could afford it, he should be allowed to take some courses at a university. Only Herman could have persuaded the old man, and it was agreed: Edwin would attend Harvard as a special student.

His two years in Cambridge were a godsend. This was the Harvard of Josiah Royce, Francis James Child, and William James, among others, and the young philosopher and poet George Santayana and his circle, which included Trumbull Stickney. Although Robinson did not take a course from James and it is uncertain whether or how well he knew Santayana and Stickney, his time at Harvard opened to him an immense horizon, a larger world in which it was neither freakish nor disgraceful to be a poet and intellectual. He gained a certain confidence and sophistication, not so much from his course work—he was still not an apt student, finding Royce's lectures incomprehensible and Anglo-Saxon too difficult—as from the ambiance of the place. As he wrote to a friend toward the end of his studies there, "Sometimes I try to imagine the state my mind would be in had I never come here, but I cannot. I feel that I have got comparatively little from my two years, but still, more than I could get in Gardiner if I lived a century." He was still an outsider—a boy from a hick town up country, without money, family, or connections—but he did make a few lifelong friends, among them his classmate and rival, the poet William Vaughan Moody, whose star shone rather more brightly in those days. He became something of a bohemian. He went avidly to the theater and the opera; he drank a good deal of beer; and he explored Boston, going once or twice, in the company of friends, to a brothel. This experience, he later said, brought home to him for the first time the debasement and servitude to which women could be subjected, and he would never forget it (although it is possible that in the painful solitude of his later years he may have resorted to an occasional visit to one of the New York houses).

Before his first year at Harvard was over, Robinson had to return home to look after his dying father. Old Edward had declined rapidly after letting go of his business affairs: he was drinking—a weakness that all the Robinson men shared—and obsessed with spiritualism. Although it is unclear whether they were actual phenomena or phantasms, and to what extent Robinson credited any of it, there were table rappings and levitations and other strange incidents that seemed to be the work of a poltergeist. In any case, he wrote to a friend that those last months "were a living hell." His father died in July, and in the fall Robinson returned to Cambridge.

His college education came to an abrupt end the following spring. In the panic and depression of 1893, land prices plummeted and the larger part of the family money was lost. For all his confidence, Herman was not prudent or canny or lucky enough to weather the hard times; he grew desperate, and he too was beginning to drink hard. Edwin came back to Gardiner and took up where he had left off, tending the two acres of vegetables, chopping wood, doing other chores, and working long hours at his poetry. Around this time, a magazine accepted and paid a pittance for a sonnet (although it did not print it for years); for the next ten or twelve years, he made not one cent from anything he wrote.

Robinson was coming to poetic maturity in what must have

been the bleakest period in the history of our poetry. If the reader has not read much American poetry of the late nineteenth century, he can have little idea what a fetid swamp it is—the sort of poetry that John Lucas has called "native hayseed and imported Pre-Raphaelitism," (and Huck Finn called "tears and flapdoodle"). Here are a few lines from Richard Watson Gilder, one of the luminaries of the time:

> What is a sonnet? 'T is the tear that fell
> From a great poet's hidden ecstacy;
> A two-edged sword, a star, a song—ah me!
> Sometimes a heavy-tolling funeral bell.

Ah me, indeed. And here is Ella Wheeler Wilcox, author of *Poems of Passion, Poems of Pleasure, Poems of Power,* and *Poems of Problems:*

> Alone it stands in Poesy's fair land,
> A temple by the muses set apart;
> A perfect structure of consummate art,
> By artists builded and by genius planned.

These inept sonneteers were addicted to writing sonnets about the sonnet. Here is Rose Hartwick Thorpe, another esteemed poet now long forgotten, on another subject:

> England's sun was slowly setting o'er the hill-tops far away,
> Filling all the land with beauty at the close of one sad day;

And the metrically challenged Richard Hovey:

> The fervid breath of our flushed Southern May
> Is sweet upon the city's throat and lips
> As a lover whose tired arm slips
> Listlessly over the shoulder of a queen.

Enough. I will spare you the saccharine pieties of Father Tabb, I will spare you Louise Imogen Guiney, Lizette Woodworth Reese, Albery Allson Whitman, and Clinton Scollard, all of them the authors of popular and respected volumes. Admittedly, there were a few poets who did not write always in this dreary, flowery dead language about trivial and unreal subjects—the aforementioned Sarah Morgan Piatt; the astringent and ill-starred Ambrose Bierce; and Robinson's Harvard contemporary, Trumbull Stickney, a marvelous talent who, had he not died at thirty, might have done great things. The rest was darkness. In 1894 and 1895, Robinson, still in his mid-twenties, was writing such poems as "Reuben Bright," "Horace to Leuconoë," "The Tavern," "The House on the Hill," "Luke Havergal" and this sonnet, "The Clerks":

> I did not think that I should find them there
> When I came back again; but there they stood,
> As in the days they dreamed of when young blood
> Was in their cheeks and women called them fair.
> Be sure, they met me with an ancient air,—
> And yes, there was a shop-worn brotherhood
> About them; but the men were just as good,
> And just as human as they ever were.
>
> And you that ache so much to be sublime,
> And you that feed yourselves with your descent,
> What comes of all your visions and your fears?
> Poets and kings are but the clerks of Time,
> Tiering the same dull webs of discontent,
> Clipping the same sad alnage of the years.

Robinson was the only poet of the 1890s to survive. Stickney, Moody, and the rest faded into oblivion, "killed," said Santayana, "by the lack of air to breathe." In 1895, young Robinson was the greatest living American poet, our first *modern* poet, and, outside of a few friends, no one knew his name. As he said, looking back many years later, "I did not exist."

The following year, his mother died a horrible death from black diphtheria. Neither the physician, the preacher, nor the undertaker was willing to come near her—the preacher said the final prayers standing out on the porch. It was left to her three sons to nurse her during her last days, to put her in her coffin, drive the wagon to the cemetery, and bury her. She did not live to see Robinson's first book, *The Torrent and the Night Before,* the publication of which he had paid for himself and which appeared little more than a week after her death.

People have exaggerated his early failures somewhat. Donald Justice has pointed out that most of the academic and literary men and women to whom he sent copies of *The Torrent and the Night Before* responded with praise; and there were at least eighteen reviews, most of them good. But this recognition of his accomplishment by a few cultivated readers did not translate into any public notice; his great distinction was, as it were, a well-kept secret.

In 1897, some of the dwindling inheritance was invested, in Dean's name, in the stock of a local drugstore. It was a popular store and flourished for a while, but the real purpose of the investment must have been to keep Dean supplied with the daily morphine he required. During this time, the friction between Herman and Edwin was intensifying. In all fairness, it had to be very hard for Herman, particularly after his catastrophic comedown in the world, to see his younger brother mooning soulfully after his wife; Emma, increasingly unhappy with Herman, no doubt took some comfort in her brother-in-law's affection and sympathy. In the fall of 1897, after a loud argument with Herman, overheard by Emma and the children, Robinson left Gardiner for good. At first he stayed with an old friend in Winthrop, across the Kennebec River, then went to Boston and Cambridge for a while, and at last to New York City, "the town down the river," establishing what would be his living arrangements for the rest of his life—renting hall bedrooms in cheap hotels and rooming houses or staying with friends, a week here, a month there, in Manhattan and Brooklyn and Staten Island, in Cambridge and Boston. Some of his friends were as poor as he, some moneyed, but Robinson, who inspired deep affection and loyalty in both men and women, was always welcome. Later in the fall of this year appeared a revised version, with some poems added and some dropped, of his first book, under the title *The Children of the Night*; this also was a vanity publication.

A little before leaving, Robinson was befriended by the two leading families of Gardiner, the Richardses and the Gardiners, related to each other—rich, land-owning Brahmins, the lords and ladies of the manor, so to speak. Mrs. Laura Richards, the daughter of Julia Ward Howe and a successful author of children's books, welcomed Robinson warmly into her family circle. These friendships, especially with her and with John Hays Gardiner, both of them great admirers of his poetry, would be invaluable to him in future years—at times, his salvation.

In 1899, Robinson was briefly a sort of office boy at Harvard—a rather humiliating experience. Less than a year later, Dean died by his own hand, of an overdose of morphine, and the ruin of the family was almost complete. It is hard to imagine what Herman and Emma, now with three daughters, were living on; probably they were helped out a little by her father. Herman was now a pathetic drunk, and around this time he moved out of the house. He was sometimes seen peddling lobsters in the Gardiner market.

During his first years in New York, Robinson was poor, but not quite destitute: what was left of his inheritance afforded him about six hundred dollars a year, enough for a young man living modestly in a bohemian milieu. His expenses were few;

his only need beyond food, lodging, a little clothing, and the occasional opera ticket, was for whiskey, which he was now consuming in large quantities. In 1900, the money began to run out; a last check in November of 1901 was for twelve dollars; his total income for that year had been less than three hundred dollars. He was now and for the next four years in dire straits—penniless, living on the free lunch in saloons, the forbearance of pitying landlords, and small loans from friends. One night in a cheap diner, he looked so woeful, shabby, and forlorn that the waiter offered to lend him two dollars.

In 1902, Robinson's next book, *Captain Craig*, was recommended to Houghton Mifflin by Moody and others, but the publisher agreed to accept it only if the costs could be guaranteed. Laura Richards and Hays Gardiner were the guarantors, and the volume was published. The response was, if anything, even quieter than the reception accorded his first book: there were a few reviews, some of them good, but his audience was still very small. Trumbull Stickney, in *The Harvard Advocate*, offered perhaps the most unstinting praise: "The honesty and simplicity of his mind, the pathos and kindness of his heart, above all the humor with which his imagination is lighted up continually, have made me begin life over again and feel once more that poetry is part of it, nay the truth of it."

In 1903, the family house in Gardiner was sold, but there is no record of Robinson's having received his share of the modest proceeds. Emma's father died, his estate almost depleted; Herman was barely able to look after himself. Emma was now supporting her mother and children on the little her father had left, sewing to make ends meet. Robinson himself was at the end of his rope; close to starvation, he took a miserable job underground as a time checker in the New York subway, then under construction, working ten hours a day for twenty cents an hour. At night he drank himself into a stupor or went out with a few friends, making the rounds of the bars—"shopping," as he called it. He wrote almost nothing that year except cheerful letters to his friends—as always, he bore his hard circumstances with stoical acceptance and humor, and of course whiskey.

In the spring of 1905, his luck began to change. He sold one poem to a magazine, the first money he had earned from his poetry in ten years—and a good omen: a week or so later, he received a letter, which read:

> My dear Mr. Robinson:
>
> I have enjoyed your poems, especially "The Children of the Night," so much that I must write to tell you so. Will you permit me to ask what you are doing and how you are getting along? I wish I could see you.
>
> Sincerely yours,
> Theodore Roosevelt

Henry Howe Richards, who was teaching at Groton, had passed on his enthusiasm for Robinson's poems to his students, one of whom was Kermit Roosevelt, the President's son, and Kermit had sent *The Children of the Night* to his father. The President read some of the poems aloud at one of his cabinet meetings, no doubt to the astonishment of the secretaries; he invited Robinson to the White House, where they talked for a long time; and he wrote and published a review of *The Children of the Night,* for which he was roundly lambasted by political enemies and turf-jealous literati. He offered Robinson a government job in Montreal and then in Mexico City, both of which Robinson refused; he did not want to leave New York. Roosevelt almost had to beg him to be allowed to help: "Will you let me know what kind of place it is that you could accept?" In the end Robinson agreed to a position in the New York Custom House as a "special agent of the Treasury," at an annual salary of two thousand dollars. It was understood by everyone that this was a sinecure; Robinson's job was to write poetry. He went to the Custom House every morning, read the newspaper, folded it neatly on his desk, and left. I cannot think of another American president who has been so disinterestedly generous to a great writer. (True, Franklin Pierce did appoint Hawthorne consul in Liverpool, but the two had been classmates and friends at Bowdoin, and the consulate was Hawthorne's reward for having written Pierce's campaign biography. And Hawthorne had to perform his duties.) During the next four years Robinson wrote very little poetry, but he was able to send a large part of his salary to Emma and his nieces. He did write two plays, *Van Zorn* and *The Porcupine*, in the vain hope of making a little money and attracting some attention; they were neither produced nor published.

If some of the stories that Chard Powers Smith relates in his biography, *Where the Light Falls*, are questionable (although to his credit he is prompt to admit that one event or another may be part of what he calls the Legend and the Dissenting Legend), there can be little doubt that Robinson was hopelessly in love with Emma and remained in that pitiable condition all his life. It is not possible to know for certain whether she loved him in return: her youngest daughter claimed she did not; the eldest insisted that she did—it is not likely we shall ever discover the truth. Without a doubt she respected and admired and liked him, and very likely she was flattered by the intensity of his attachment; but whatever her feelings, it is clear that no one could ever wholly replace her reprobate husband in her heart. Although Robinson's failure to win her was an unhealing and painful wound, he may well have profited from this long experience of unrequited love. What it took from his life, it gave back abundantly to his art—Emma, or rather the love triangle (as Robinson perceived it) consisting of himself and her and Herman, appears continually in his work, in scores of short poems, in *Lancelot* and *Merlin* and in most of the other long poems.

As for other women, there seem to have been none. Many women in the literary circles of the day were attracted to him, teased him, and flirted with him at one time or another, but apparently without success. The dancer Isadora Duncan offered him her favors, which he politely refused. Several of his friends claimed he was celibate, but when Ridgely Torrance, one of his intimates, heard that, he laughed. The reader may make of this what he will. But if Robinson had any erotic life after his Harvard years, it must have been very limited.

Robinson saw his brother from time to time, in New York or Boston, sometimes on the street. Although Herman had made a serious attempt to stop drinking, he was in bad shape: only in his forties, he looked like an old man. In 1908 he died in a ward of the Boston City Hospital. That same year, William Howard Taft became president. Under the incoming administration, the poet was expected to perform his duties at the Custom House; since he had no idea what those duties consisted of, he resigned. For the next five or six years, he composed very little verse. He was writing fiction, for which he had no talent, and like the plays, it was ignored. He was drinking heavily again and sinking back once more into desperate poverty. In 1910, *The Town Down the River* appeared, his first independent commercial publication but his weakest book thus far, containing at most half a dozen good poems and only one of the great ones—"For a Dead Lady," an elegy for his mother.

By 1911, Robinson was again surviving on loans and the hospitality of friends; Hays Gardiner, now a professor emeritus at Harvard, was probably helping him. Of such patronage, Malcolm Cowley has written, "The gifts he received . . . didn't wound his Yankee pride because he felt that they were being given, not to him, but through him to poetry. Having taken vows of poverty, chastity, and obedience to his art, he could accept charity as if he were a whole monastic order." He was a hard case. He refused to teach, to give readings or lectures, to write reviews. It was in this year that the young writer Hermann Hagedorn (who would later write the first full-scale biography of the poet) persuaded him, against his better judgment, to visit the newly opened MacDowell Colony in New Hampshire (established by Marian MacDowell, the composer's widow, one of the great private benefactors of the arts in this century). Robinson was extremely suspicious of anything called a "colony," but once he got to Peterborough and was given a cabin in the woods with a view of Mount Monadnock, he quickly changed his mind. He loved the place, and he would go up there every summer for the next twenty-three years. He went on doggedly writing his unsaleable prose for another year or so, but despite the free summers in Peterborough, he was broke and half starved again—as he said, "on my uppers—absolutely." He had been borrowing from friends till he could borrow no more, when, in 1913, Hays Gardiner died, leaving him a legacy of four thousand dollars. Robinson said, "At the rate I was spending money just then, I could have lived for a million years on four thousand dollars."

His life began to change. He stopped drinking (and would stay on the wagon until the 18th Amendment became law, when he took up whiskey again in protest) and was once more writing poems. He was now at the very height of his powers; these were the years in which he wrote eleven or twelve masterpieces, including "Eros Turannos," "Veteran Sirens," "The Poor Relation" and "Hillcrest," and, a little later, "The Wandering Jew." If he had written nothing but these poems, he would still have to be considered one of our greatest poets. Every May he went up to the MacDowell Colony, where he was regarded by the younger artists with awe and affection and the deference due a great man, though he rarely played the part. Of his fellow colonists over the years, some of the most notable were Padraic and Mary Colum, Thornton

Wilder, Maxwell Bodenheim, Elinor Wylie, Percy Mackaye, and Ridgely Torrance—the last two became his fast friends. After his four or five free months in New Hampshire, he would spend the autumn and winter moving between Boston and New York, from one friend's house to another. He was just beginning to be widely known. He already had some reputation in France, where the scholar Charles Cestre had been writing about his work, while in New York, the great Spanish poet Juan Ramón Jiménez and his wife, Zenobia, were reading him and had chosen a number of poems from *The Man Against the Sky* (1916) to translate, including "Hillcrest," "Bokardo" and "Another Dark Lady." In 1917, he received from the New York Trust Company the first of four annual payments of twelve hundred dollars, a subsidy raised anonymously by some of his affluent friends. (Robinson knew who they were and eventually paid them all back, giving them some valuable manuscripts in addition.) In 1921, his *Collected Poems* won the Pulitzer Prize, the first of three he would win. Over the next few years, he wrote a number of his finest short poems, such as "Mr. Flood's Party," "Lost Anchors," "Many Are Called," and "The Sheaves"—but almost none after 1924: the short poems, he said, no longer came. For the last ten or eleven years of his life, he worked almost exclusively on the book-length poems, some of them popular at the time, but now little read.

In 1925, Robinson had a decisive meeting with Emma, during which, it is said, she made it clear once and for all that he must abandon all hope of marrying her. She may well have known what Robinson himself did not know, that he could not marry anyone. Vocation and long habit had made him an inveterate bachelor—and there may have been another, deeper reason. Robert Frost, in a perceptive letter to a friend, wrote, "I am not the Platonist Robinson was. By Platonist I mean one who believes what we have here is an imperfect copy of what is in heaven. The woman you have is an imperfect copy of some woman in heaven or in someone else's bed. . . . A truly gallant Platonist will remain a bachelor as Robinson did from unwillingness to reduce any woman to the condition of being used without being idolized." He never went back to Gardiner.

He was "doctored" by Yale and Bowdoin, as he put it, and there were other invitations, but the one that really would have pleased him never came. The support of a few professors and the private persuasion of some influential friends were to no avail—Harvard was giving its honorary degrees to Andrew Mellon and J. Pierpont Morgan, men like that. And this was sadly fitting in its way, for the Morgans and Mellons stood for everything Robinson abhorred in American life.

Toward the end of the twenties, his health, which had never been robust, was beginning to fail. In 1927, *Tristram,* the last of his long Arthurian poems, won a Pulitzer Prize and over the next few years sold over one hundred thousand copies; Robinson was for the first time making substantial sums of money, some of which he gave to the Gardiner hospital for a diagnostic lab in memory of Dean. Over the next six or seven years, making the most of his declining energies, he wrote and published another six book-length poems (the best of which, in my opinion, is *The Man Who Died Twice*). He suffered from intermittent depression, for which he was treated by the well-known poet-psychiatrist Merrill Moore. Despite his now comfortable income, his way of life did not change radically from the way he had been living for decades, except that now he could play the stock market a little and he could give money to friends who needed it.

In January 1935, feeling worse than usual, he was admitted to New York Hospital, where an exploratory operation revealed inoperable pancreatic cancer. Even on his deathbed in the early spring of 1935, Robinson lost none of his passionate commitment to his art nor his intense and continuous sympathy for others. Exhausted, weak, and in pain, he patiently corrected proofs for his final book, *King Jasper*. And from his hospital window he would look down at Welfare Island, as it was then called, and pity the poor wretches in prison and in the city hospital below.

Considering his many sufferings and ordeals, the agonies caused by the damage to his ear, his beloved Dean's addiction and early death, his lifelong yearning for Emma, his mother's terrifying last days, the many years of impoverished loneliness, of being unknown and going unread, Herman's heartbreaking end, and so much more, it is a little startling, and yet wholly in character, that he could say, not long before he died, "As lives go, my own life would be called, and properly, a rather fortunate one."

II

What has happened to Edwin Arlington Robinson? When I was a young student at Kenyon in the early fifties, reading his poems with John Crowe Ransom and the ardent Denham Sutcliffe (who would later edit a volume of his letters), I took it for granted that he was unquestionably one of the great American poets. So did my fellow students. He was one of James Wright's literary saints. We were deeply affected by those poems—we read them aloud, got them by heart, talked and argued about them. It must have been the case, even then, that our opinion was not unquestionable and certainly not general, but it was fifteen or twenty years before I began to realize that for most people, both in the literary world and in the universities, Robinson had become almost a nonperson. I can remember James Wright in the late sixties sadly musing on the neglect into which Robinson's work had fallen; and sometime in the seventies Irving Howe wrote, "The centennial of Edwin Arlington Robinson passed several years ago—he was born on December 22, 1869—with barely a murmur of public notice. There were a few academic volumes of varying merit, but no recognition in our larger journals and reviews, for Robinson seems the kind of poet who is likely to remain permanently out of fashion." In the years since then, that darkness has only deepened. Except for recent essays by Donald Hall and Donald Justice (from which I have quoted in the note to "Eros Turannos"), I can scarcely recall the last time I saw Robinson written of with intelligence and love. The Modern Languages Association have told me they have no records of such things, but I would guess it has been two or three decades, if not more, since a member last presented a paper or arranged a symposium on Robinson at one of their conventions. In 1996, a few scholars and devoted readers, organized by Mark Melnicove, put on the first of two festivals in Gardiner, Maine—Donald Justice and I were there, and Rachel Hadas and others, and it made quite a stir, but as far as I know, the stir was largely confined to Gardiner. A few years back, there was a series of documentaries on PBS on the lives and works of what the producers (or more likely, Helen Vendler, the presiding critic) took to be the thirteen greatest American poets—thirteen, but E. A. Robinson was not one of them. One after another, the beautiful volumes of the Library of America roll off the presses—Stowe and Stein and Steinbeck, Baldwin and Chandler and London—all of them worthy enough, but none anywhere near Robinson in artistic power and importance. Not very long ago, in a college bookstore, I came across a hefty new multicultural anthology of American poetry which seemed to include every poeticule from Edward Coote Pinkney to Audre Lorde, but not a single poem by Robinson; not one. Other anthologies are not much better. Most often they will include a token poem, almost inevitably the slight but very famous one that Donald Hall has described as "a brief story in quatrains, punchy as a television ad, in which the protagonist surprises us (once) by putting a bullet through his head." A few other poems, occasionally some good ones, have been "pickled in anthological brine" (as Robinson liked to say), but you would be far more likely to find "Miniver Cheevy" or "The Mill" than, say, "Veteran Sirens" or "The Wandering Jew." In one huge anthology widely used in the colleges, Robinson is given five pages—about the same amount of space as E. J. Pratt and Charles Olson, and much less than William Everson, less than Rich, less than Ammons and Ginsberg. That is merely embarrassing; but his *Collected Poems* have been out of print for a good many years, and that is a national disgrace.

How can such a thing have happened? How are we to account for this state of affairs, that one of the greatest poets to have emerged in this country, a poet worthy to be in the company of Emerson, Dickinson, Stevens, and Frost, should be so little read, so little celebrated? Many explanations have been offered, and if there is some truth to all of them, no one explanation can suffice.

It must be in part that Robinson wrote in meter and rhyme, wrote to be understood, and took for gospel that reason was surely one of the constituents of poetry—"the old-fashioned way to be new"—and there is still, among far too many readers, teachers, reviewers, and poets, a stubborn prejudice against metrical verse and against clear rational procedure. Even in the universities, of all places, there are people who regard reason as a form of tyranny or torture. We live, as Yvor Winters has written, in an age "which is convinced that thought and poetry are mutually destructive, that rational structure is a defect in a poem rather than a virtue, that genuine poetry must be confused to express a confused period. . . ." One of our most lionized poets, a former laureate, claims that "accentual-syllabics are the principal way in which the educated classes in Europe mystified their utter-

ance and gave it repressive authority, which they called po-
etry"; and sad to say, this kind of ignorant cant is not uncom-
mon. A good reader of Robinson, as of most poetry, ought to
be reasonably at home in and alert to the metrical conventions
and the subtle uses poets can put them to, and there are not as
many such readers as there once were.

There are other qualities of Robinson's work that contem-
porary readers are not accustomed to and perhaps dislike, or
think they dislike, and so have no inkling of how much plea-
sure they might find in his poems. Louis Coxe has said that
Robinson is "spare where we are lush, general where we are
specific, detailed where we are reticent and silent." His dic-
tion tends to be abstract and his sensory detail sparse, and
since we were taught and taught that we must go in fear of ab-
stractions, many people have by now forgotten how precise
and witty, and even moving, an abstract diction can be, how
much eloquence and power can lie in the plain style, in bal-
ance and decorum, in a quiet, restrained voice. And Robinson
embodied in his work as in his life virtues that are not very
highly regarded nowadays: moderation, self-control and self-
knowledge, moral seriousness, the recognition of limits and of
limitations, the tragic view of life as a fate to be accepted and
endured with stoic courage. Our taste and bias are still mostly
for the romantic and sensational, the dazzling and difficult,
whereas Robinson was and thought of himself as essentially a
classicist. Most of our famous contemporary poets are true-
blue Romantics and Emersonians at heart, but Robinson,
though he loved Emerson's poetry, is not; he absorbed and re-
constructed for himself most of what was left of the old and
desiccated Puritan tradition, and I would say there is more of
the sin-obsessed but merciful Jonathan Edwards in him than
of Emerson. Donald Justice has suggested that his poetry
might not seem challenging or daring enough for readers in

our time and that his style has gone out of fashion. And not merely his style: Justice goes on to say, "Pieties there still are in Robinson, and this is surely one of the reasons for the undeniable decline of his reputation, since even Robinson's darker pieties have by now inevitably become those of a vanished past."

There are a few other reasons worth mentioning. Robinson belonged to no coterie or movement and had no talent for self-promotion; he had nothing of Pound's gift, or Ginsberg's, for publicity and notoriety—and even if he had known how to operate the levers of advancement, he would have refrained. Although he modernized himself very early, before Frost did, and long before Pound and Eliot did, he did it very quietly, not thinking of himself as in any way revolutionary. In several superficial ways he might have struck his few readers as not very different from the other poets of his era; we of course can now see clearly that the difference is enormous— it is the difference between very bad and very great poetry. Then, too, there is the awkward accident of his dates. We tend to forget he was not contemporary with Pound and Eliot, but a generation older; *his* contemporaries were Kipling and Masters, Dowson and Stephen Crane. His first book appeared in 1896, the same year that *A Shropshire Lad* was published, two years before Hardy's first book of poems. Edwin Fussell has put it astutely: "Because he is the only major American poet of his own generation and because his early work seems to anticipate the 'new poetry,' he often suffers a unique injustice: first he is grouped with much younger poets and then, in comparison with them, he is damned as 'too traditional.' " By the time the great period of modernist literature was in full swing, most of his best work was behind him. As he himself said, shortly before his death, "I must be very far behind the times. Once I was so modern that people wouldn't have me."

And there is no denying that he published far too much. Although he had occasionally had great success with blank verse poems of middle length—roughly two hundred to four hundred lines—his genius was for the short rhymed poem, and by 1924 or so, that vein had pretty well run dry. The rest of his life was given over to the composition of the book-length poems, novels in verse, which, though they have their moments, most readers have found tedious. He had earlier written his two best long poems, *Merlin* and *Lancelot,* profound explorations of human love, studded with passages of intense beauty and power; but even they seem much too long for narratives that contain an immense amount of conversation and very little action. (Even Frost, who deeply admired much of Robinson's work, remarked, "This later stuff ... I can't see how he can stay awake writing it.") I believe Robinson knew that the short poems were his great achievement, but he really had no choice in the matter: they did not come any more, he said, and he could only do what was given him to do. Then, too, he had had to endure years of poverty and near starvation in order to practice his art, and had many times accepted help from many friends; he owed it both to them and to himself to go on turning out books of verse. As Cunningham wrote, "The professed poet must keep writing, 'scrivening to the end against his fate' for it is the justification of his life. So he wrote too much, and when written out he could not swear off."

He was often praised for his weakest work, especially during his brief period of fame, from 1921 when his *Collected Poems* won his first Pulitzer Prize until his death in 1935. Ironically, this was the very period in which the Modernists were much in the public eye and their growing dominance would soon begin to overshadow Robinson's reputation. *Tristram,* the third and flabbiest of his Arthurian poems, which Louis Coxe calls his only meretricious performance, and "one which seems written for a woman's magazine," was consciously intended to be a great popular success, and it was; it won the Pulitzer and sold more than fifty thousand copies in the first year. Indeed, it was so popular that Robinson himself grew embarrassed by the praise; he had to know that it was far from his best work. And it is almost always the case that undeserved and too lavish praise will produce a strong reaction. That reaction when it came surely contributed to the rapid decline of Robinson's reputation after his death a few years later.

But I would suggest that the primary reason for the neglect of this great poet has to do with the life he wrote about and the way he saw it. It is generally acknowledged that American poetry before Robinson took little if any notice of ordinary men and women; as Irving Howe has written, "Robinson was the first American poet of stature to bring commonplace people and commonplace experience into our poetry. Whitman had invoked such people and even rhapsodized over them, but as individual creatures with warm blood they are not really to be found in his pages." And the men and women Robinson writes about are not the happier people of their time. They are the losers in the race—the penniless maiden aunts, unregenerate skirt chasers, betrayed wives and suicides, the solitary drunk who has outlived his cronies, the wastrel, the miser and the fraud, the prostitute, the black sheep—and Robinson knows them; some of them are aspects of himself. Yet at the same time he knows that their lives, like any lives, are finally unknowable, that every person in his inmost being is a mystery to others, even to himself. Robinson's people were also the casualties of a nation hell-bent on empire, expansion, and the accumulation of capital, a society corrupted by pride and greed, heedlessly violating "the merciless old verities," a culture in which personal ambition, boosterism, the cash nexus had taken the place of community and the serious life of the spirit—everything that Robinson detested and feared and summed up in the one word *materialism.* He does not presume to speak for the injured and insulted, the alienated and outcast; they themselves often have little idea what they want to say. All he can do is to imagine and meditate on the shapes of their small tragedies and tell honestly and accurately what he sees, not concealing his deep conviction that he can never know the reality of these mute and damaged lives, nor can we. He can not account for them; all he can do is lament them and insist on their dignity. And beneath it all is the existential solitude of every human soul, what Robinson calls "the blank taste of time," and which he evokes more deeply and feelingly than almost any other poet. This is not a recipe for popularity.

I have the impression that the younger academic critics and scholars are not really very interested in the characters who inhabit Robinson's poems. The intelligentsia seem to come to poetry with a whole set of preconceptions and ideologies and theories, and I suspect that most of them are simply bored or exasperated by someone like Robinson, this long-dead white male who has no politics, no grievances, no illusion that he can speak for other people or that his poems can lighten or mitigate their unhappiness. Perhaps I am being unfair. It may simply be that the intellectuals and tastemakers are very much like the people outside of universities—like most of us—who would just as soon not face the implications of these poems, the unpalatable truths they seem to contain, although the poet denies that he knows the truth about anything. But the world he depicts with so much accuracy and clarity is a world all too much like ours, in which people cannot go on living without hope but in which hope is little more than wishful thinking or self-deception—the world that lies just beneath the laugh track, the games and spectacles, the endless distraction and frivolity with which we are always trying to ward off or ignore the starker realities. (Not very long ago, educators in Maine demanded that "Richard Cory" be removed from the Maine Educational Assessment Test, on the grounds that it was too depressing and that it condoned suicide!) James Wright said that Robinson goes unread because he is a serious man. Winters' diagnosis is an even harsher indictment of our society, perhaps of any civilized society: he declared that Robinson's style "is accurate with the conscientiousness of genius, and such accuracy is invariably a major obstacle to success. Nothing baffles the average critic so completely as honesty—he is prepared for everything but that; and I have the impression that this has been true in every period."

Robinson is preëminently the poet of the subjunctive mood. He was enough of a Puritan and classicist to believe there *is* such a thing as truth, and that it was his duty to seek it and to set down what he saw and thought, as soberly and accurately as he could; but he was also honest and wise enough to understand that truth is shifting and many-shaded, "circumstanced with dark and doubt"—and in the end, not given to the human mind to know, except now and then in fleeting intuitions, faint gleams. That may be why he seems in so many of his poems to be on the brink of revealing something of great moment that is never actually revealed, but always deferred, withheld, obscured. And yet, in his great poems, this is somehow not cause for frustration, impatience, or bewilderment, but rather for gratitude, assent, and a serene satisfaction. How can this be? It may be as Borges has suggested: "Music, states of happiness, mythology, faces belabored by time, certain sunsets and certain places, are trying to tell us something, or have told us something we should not have missed, or are about to tell us something. This imminence of a revelation which does not take place is, perhaps, the æsthetic experience." And it may be that Edwin Arlington Robinson understood this very well himself, dealing as he did, again and

again, with the imminent but suspended and unspoken, the al-
most but not quite hinted,

> And with a mighty meaning of a kind
> That tells the more the more it is not told.

—ROBERT MEZEY

From

THE CHILDREN
OF THE
NIGHT

LUKE HAVERGAL

Go to the western gate, Luke Havergal,
There where the vines cling crimson on the wall,
And in the twilight wait for what will come.
The leaves will whisper there of her, and some,
Like flying words, will strike you as they fall;
But go, and if you listen she will call.
Go to the western gate, Luke Havergal—
Luke Havergal.

No, there is not a dawn in eastern skies
To rift the fiery night that's in your eyes;
But there, where western glooms are gathering,
The dark will end the dark, if anything:
God slays Himself with every leaf that flies,
And hell is more than half of paradise.
No, there is not a dawn in eastern skies—
In eastern skies.

Out of a grave I come to tell you this,
Out of a grave I come to quench the kiss
That flames upon your forehead with a glow
That blinds you to the way that you must go.
Yes, there is yet one way to where she is,
Bitter, but one that faith may never miss.
Out of a grave I come to tell you this—
To tell you this.

There is the western gate, Luke Havergal,
There are the crimson leaves upon the wall.
Go, for the winds are tearing them away,—
Nor think to riddle the dead words they say,
Nor any more to feel them as they fall;
But go, and if you trust her she will call.
There is the western gate, Luke Havergal—
Luke Havergal.

JOHN EVERELDOWN

"Where are you going to-night, to-night,—
  Where are you going, John Evereldown?
There's never the sign of a star in sight,
  Nor a lamp that's nearer than Tilbury Town.
Why do you stare as a dead man might?
Where are you pointing away from the light?
And where are you going to-night, to-night,—
  Where are you going, John Evereldown?"

"Right through the forest, where none can see,
  There's where I'm going, to Tilbury Town.
The men are asleep,—or awake, may be,—
  But the women are calling John Evereldown.
Ever and ever they call for me,
And while they call can a man be free?
So right through the forest, where none can see,
  There's where I'm going, to Tilbury Town."

"But why are you going so late, so late,—
  Why are you going, John Evereldown?
Though the road be smooth and the way be straight,
  There are two long leagues to Tilbury Town.
Come in by the fire, old man, and wait!
Why do you chatter out there by the gate?
And why are you going so late, so late,—
  Why are you going, John Evereldown?"

"I follow the women wherever they call,—
    That's why I'm going to Tilbury Town.
God knows if I pray to be done with it all,
    But God is no friend to John Evereldown.
So the clouds may come and the rain may fall,
The shadows may creep and the dead men crawl,—
But I follow the women wherever they call,
    And that's why I'm going to Tilbury Town."

THE HOUSE ON THE HILL

They are all gone away,
    The House is shut and still,
There is nothing more to say.

Through broken walls and gray
    The winds blow bleak and shrill:
They are all gone away.

Nor is there one to-day
    To speak them good or ill:
There is nothing more to say.

Why is it then we stray
    Around the sunken sill?
They are all gone away,

And our poor fancy-play
    For them is wasted skill:
There is nothing more to say.

There is ruin and decay
    In the House on the Hill:
They are all gone away,
There is nothing more to say.

RICHARD CORY

Whenever Richard Cory went down town,
We people on the pavement looked at him:
He was a gentleman from sole to crown,
Clean favored, and imperially slim.

And he was always quietly arrayed,
And he was always human when he talked;
But still he fluttered pulses when he said,
"Good-morning," and he glittered when he walked.

And he was rich—yes, richer than a king—
And admirably schooled in every grace:
In fine, we thought that he was everything
To make us wish that we were in his place.

So on we worked, and waited for the light,
And went without the meat, and cursed the bread;
And Richard Cory, one calm summer night,
Went home and put a bullet through his head.

DEAR FRIENDS

Dear friends, reproach me not for what I do,
Nor counsel me, nor pity me; nor say
That I am wearing half my life away
For bubble-work that only fools pursue.
And if my bubbles be too small for you,
Blow bigger then your own: the games we play
To fill the frittered minutes of a day,
Good glasses are to read the spirit through.

And whoso reads may get him some shrewd skill;
And some unprofitable scorn resign,
To praise the very thing that he deplores;
So, friends (dear friends), remember, if you will,
The shame I win for singing is all mine,
The gold I miss for dreaming is all yours.

THE STORY OF THE ASHES
AND THE FLAME

No matter why, nor whence, nor when she came,
There was her place. No matter what men said,
No matter what she was; living or dead,
Faithful or not, he loved her all the same.
The story was as old as human shame,
But ever since that lonely night she fled,
With books to blind him, he had only read
The story of the ashes and the flame.

There she was always coming pretty soon
To fool him back, with penitent scared eyes
That had in them the laughter of the moon
For baffled lovers, and to make him think—
Before she gave him time enough to wink—
Her kisses were the keys to Paradise.

ZOLA

Because he puts the compromising chart
Of hell before your eyes, you are afraid;
Because he counts the price that you have paid
For innocence, and counts it from the start,
You loathe him. But he sees the human heart
Of God meanwhile, and in His hand was weighed
Your squeamish and emasculate crusade
Against the grim dominion of his art.

Never until we conquer the uncouth
Connivings of our shamed indifference
(We call it Christian faith) are we to scan
The racked and shrieking hideousness of Truth
To find, in hate's polluted self-defence
Throbbing, the pulse, the divine heart of man.

AARON STARK

Withal a meagre man was Aaron Stark,
Cursed and unkempt, shrewd, shrivelled, and morose.
A miser was he, with a miser's nose,
And eyes like little dollars in the dark.
His thin, pinched mouth was nothing but a mark;
And when he spoke there came like sullen blows
Through scattered fangs a few snarled words and close,
As if a cur were chary of its bark.

Glad for the murmur of his hard renown,
Year after year he shambled through the town,
A loveless exile moving with a staff;
And oftentimes there crept into his ears
A sound of alien pity, touched with tears,—
And then (and only then) did Aaron laugh.

CLIFF KLINGENHAGEN

Cliff Klingenhagen had me in to dine
With him one day; and after soup and meat,
And all the other things there were to eat,
Cliff took two glasses and filled one with wine
And one with wormwood. Then, without a sign
For me to choose at all, he took the draught
Of bitterness himself, and lightly quaffed
It off, and said the other one was mine.

And when I asked him what the deuce he meant
By doing that, he only looked at me
And smiled, and said it was a way of his.
And though I know the fellow, I have spent
Long time a-wondering when I shall be
As happy as Cliff Klingenhagen is.

THE CLERKS

I did not think that I should find them there
When I came back again; but there they stood,
As in the days they dreamed of when young blood
Was in their cheeks and women called them fair.
Be sure, they met me with an ancient air,—
And yes, there was a shop-worn brotherhood
About them; but the men were just as good,
And just as human as they ever were.

And you that ache so much to be sublime,
And you that feed yourselves with your descent,
What comes of all your visions and your fears?
Poets and kings are but the clerks of Time,
Tiering the same dull webs of discontent,
Clipping the same sad alnage of the years.

FLEMING HELPHENSTINE

At first I thought there was a superfine
Persuasion in his face; but the free glow
That filled it when he stopped and cried, "Hollo!"
Shone joyously, and so I let it shine.
He said his name was Fleming Helphenstine,
But be that as it may;—I only know
He talked of this and that and So-and-So,
And laughed and chaffed like any friend of mine.

But soon, with a queer, quick frown, he looked at me,
And I looked hard at him; and there we gazed
In a strained way that made us cringe and wince:
Then, with a wordless clogged apology
That sounded half confused and half amazed,
He dodged,—and I have never seen him since.

Thomas Hood

The man who cloaked his bitterness within
This winding-sheet of puns and pleasantries,
God never gave to look with common eyes
Upon a world of anguish and of sin:
His brother was the branded man of Lynn;
And there are woven with his jollities
The nameless and eternal tragedies
That render hope and hopelessness akin.

We laugh, and crown him; but anon we feel
A still chord sorrow-swept,—a weird unrest;
And thin dim shadows home to midnight steal,
As if the very ghost of mirth were dead—
As if the joys of time to dreams had fled,
Or sailed away with Ines to the West.

HORACE TO LEUCONOË

I pray you not, Leuconoë, to pore
With unpermitted eyes on what may be
Appointed by the gods for you and me,
Nor on Chaldean figures any more.
'T were infinitely better to implore
The present only:—whether Jove decree
More winters yet to come, or whether he
Make even this, whose hard, wave-eaten shore
Shatters the Tuscan seas to-day, the last—
Be wise withal, and rack your wine, nor fill
Your bosom with large hopes; for while I sing,
The envious close of time is narrowing;—
So seize the day, or ever it be past,
And let the morrow come for what it will.

REUBEN BRIGHT

Because he was a butcher and thereby
Did earn an honest living (and did right),
I would not have you think that Reuben Bright
Was any more a brute than you or I;
For when they told him that his wife must die,
He stared at them, and shook with grief and fright,
And cried like a great baby half that night,
And made the women cry to see him cry.

And after she was dead, and he had paid
The singers and the sexton and the rest,
He packed a lot of things that she had made
Most mournfully away in an old chest
Of hers, and put some chopped-up cedar boughs
In with them, and tore down the slaughter-house.

THE TAVERN

Whenever I go by there nowadays
And look at the rank weeds and the strange grass,
The torn blue curtains and the broken glass,
I seem to be afraid of the old place;
And something stiffens up and down my face,
For all the world as if I saw the ghost
Of old Ham Amory, the murdered host,
With his dead eyes turned on me all aglaze.

The Tavern has a story, but no man
Can tell us what it is. We only know
That once long after midnight, years ago,
A stranger galloped up from Tilbury Town,
Who brushed, and scared, and all but overran
That skirt-crazed reprobate, John Evereldown.

20 ·

GEORGE CRABBE

Give him the darkest inch your shelf allows,
Hide him in lonely garrets, if you will,—
But his hard, human pulse is throbbing still
With the sure strength that fearless truth endows.
In spite of all fine science disavows,
Of his plain excellence and stubborn skill
There yet remains what fashion cannot kill,
Though years have thinned the laurel from his brows.

Whether or not we read him, we can feel
From time to time the vigor of his name
Against us like a finger for the shame
And emptiness of what our souls reveal
In books that are as altars where we kneel
To consecrate the flicker, not the flame.

ON THE NIGHT OF A
FRIEND'S WEDDING

If ever I am old, and all alone,
I shall have killed one grief, at any rate;
For then, thank God, I shall not have to wait
Much longer for the sheaves that I have sown.
The devil only knows what I have done,
But here I am, and here are six or eight
Good friends, who most ingenuously prate
About my songs to such and such a one.

But everything is all askew to-night,—
As if the time were come, or almost come,
For their untenanted mirage of me
To lose itself and crumble out of sight,
Like a tall ship that floats above the foam
A little while, and then breaks utterly.

VERLAINE

Why do you dig like long-clawed scavengers
To touch the covered corpse of him that fled
The uplands for the fens, and rioted
Like a sick satyr with doom's worshippers?
Come! let the grass grow there; and leave his verse
To tell the story of the life he led.
Let the man go: let the dead flesh be dead,
And let the worms be its biographers.

Song sloughs away the sin to find redress
In art's complete remembrance: nothing clings
For long but laurel to the stricken brow
That felt the Muse's finger; nothing less
Than hell's fulfilment of the end of things
Can blot the star that shines on Paris now.

FROM

OCTAVES

XI

Still through the dusk of dead, blank-legended,
And unremunerative years we search
To get where life begins, and still we groan
Because we do not find the living spark
Where no spark ever was; and thus we die,
Still searching, like poor old astronomers
Who totter off to bed and go to sleep,
To dream of untriangulated stars.

XXIII

Here by the windy docks I stand alone,
But yet companioned. There the vessel goes,
And there my friend goes with it; but the wake
That melts and ebbs between that friend and me
Love's earnest is of Life's all-purposeful
And all-triumphant sailing, when the ships
Of Wisdom loose their fretful chains and swing
Forever from the crumbled wharves of Time.

From

CAPTAIN CRAIG

ISAAC AND ARCHIBALD

(To Mrs. Henry Richards)

Isaac and Archibald were two old men.
I knew them, and I may have laughed at them
A little; but I must have honored them
For they were old, and they were good to me.

I do not think of either of them now
Without remembering, infallibly,
A journey that I made one afternoon
With Isaac to find out what Archibald
Was doing with his oats. It was high time
Those oats were cut, said Isaac; and he feared
That Archibald—well, he could never feel
Quite sure of Archibald. Accordingly
The good old man invited me—that is,
Permitted me—to go along with him;
And I, with a small boy's adhesiveness
To competent old age, got up and went.
I do not know that I cared overmuch
For Archibald's or anybody's oats,
But Archibald was quite another thing,
And Isaac yet another; and the world
Was wide, and there was gladness everywhere.
We walked together down the River Road
With all the warmth and wonder of the land
Around us, and the wayside flash of leaves,—
And Isaac said the day was glorious;
But somewhere at the end of the first mile
I found that I was figuring to find
How long those ancient legs of his would keep
The pace that he had set for them. The sun
Was hot, and I was ready to sweat blood;

But Isaac, for aught I could make of him,
Was cool to his hat-band. So I said then
With a dry gasp of affable despair,
Something about the scorching days we have
In August without knowing it sometimes;
But Isaac said the day was like a dream,
And praised the Lord, and talked about the breeze.
I made a fair confession of the breeze,
And crowded casually on his thought
The nearness of a profitable nook
That I could see. First I was half inclined
To caution him that he was growing old,
But something that was not compassion soon
Made plain the folly of all subterfuge.
Isaac was old, but not so old as that.

So I proposed, without an overture,
That we be seated in the shade a while,
And Isaac made no murmur. Soon the talk
Was turned on Archibald, and I began
To feel some premonitions of a kind
That only childhood knows; for the old man
Had looked at me and clutched me with his eye,
And asked if I had ever noticed things.
I told him that I could not think of them,
And I knew then, by the frown that left his face
Unsatisfied, that I had injured him.
"My good young friend," he said, "you cannot feel
What I have seen so long. You have the eyes—
Oh, yes—but you have not the other things:
The sight within that never will deceive,
You do not know—you have no right to know;
The twilight warning of experience,
The singular idea of loneliness,—

These are not yours. But they have long been mine,
And they have shown me now for seven years
That Archibald is changing. It is not
So much that he should come to his last hand,
And leave the game, and go the old way down;
But I have known him in and out so long,
And I have seen so much of good in him
That other men have shared and have not seen,
And I have gone so far through thick and thin,
Through cold and fire with him, that now it brings
To this old heart of mine an ache that you
Have not yet lived enough to know about.
But even unto you, and your boy's faith,
Your freedom, and your untried confidence,
A time will come to find out what it means
To know that you are losing what was yours,
To know that you are being left behind;
And then the long contempt of innocence—
God bless you, boy!—don't think the worse of it
Because an old man chatters in the shade—
Will all be like a story you have read
In childhood and remembered for the pictures.
And when the best friend of your life goes down,
When first you know in him the slackening
That comes, and coming always tells the end,—
Now in a common word that would have passed
Uncaught from any other lips than his,
Now in some trivial act of every day,
Done as he might have done it all along
But for a twinging little difference
That nips you like a squirrel's teeth—oh, yes,
Then you will understand it well enough.
But oftener it comes in other ways;
It comes without your knowing when it comes;

You know that he is changing, and you know
That he is going—just as I know now
That Archibald is going, and that I
Am staying.... Look at me, my boy,
And when the time shall come for you to see
That I must follow after him, try then
To think of me, to bring me back again,
Just as I was to-day. Think of the place
Where we are sitting now, and think of me—
Think of old Isaac as you knew him then,
When you set out with him in August once
To see old Archibald."—The words come back
Almost as Isaac must have uttered them,
And there comes with them a dry memory
Of something in my throat that would not move.

If you had asked me then to tell just why
I made so much of Isaac and the things
He said, I should have gone far for an answer;
For I knew it was not sorrow that I felt,
Whatever I may have wished it, or tried then
To make myself believe. My mouth was full
Of words, and they would have been comforting
To Isaac, spite of my twelve years, I think;
But there was not in me the willingness
To speak them out. Therefore I watched the ground;
And I was wondering what made the Lord
Create a thing so nervous as an ant,
When Isaac, with commendable unrest,
Ordained that we should take the road again—
For it was yet three miles to Archibald's,
And one to the first pump. I felt relieved
All over when the old man told me that;
I felt that he had stilled a fear of mine

That those extremities of heat and cold
Which he had long gone through with Archibald
Had made the man impervious to both;
But Isaac had a desert somewhere in him,
And at the pump he thanked God for all things
That He had put on earth for men to drink,
And he drank well,—so well that I proposed
That we go slowly lest I learn too soon
The bitterness of being left behind,
And all those other things. That was a joke
To Isaac, and it pleased him very much;
And that pleased me—for I was twelve years old.

At the end of an hour's walking after that
The cottage of old Archibald appeared.
Little and white and high on a smooth round hill
It stood, with hackmatacks and apple-trees
Before it, and a big barn-roof beyond;
And over the place—trees, houses, fields and all—
Hovered an air of still simplicity
And a fragrance of old summers—the old style
That lives the while it passes. I dare say
That I was lightly conscious of all this
When Isaac, of a sudden, stopped himself,
And for the long first quarter of a minute
Gazed with incredulous eyes, forgetful quite
Of breezes and of me and of all else
Under the scorching sun but a smooth-cut field,
Faint yellow in the distance. I was young,
But there were a few things that I could see,
And this was one of them.—"Well, well!" said he;
And "Archibald will be surprised, I think,"
Said I. But all my childhood subtlety
Was lost on Isaac, for he strode along

Like something out of Homer—powerful
And awful on the wayside, so I thought.
Also I thought how good it was to be
So near the end of my short-legged endeavor
To keep the pace with Isaac for five miles.

Hardly had we turned in from the main road
When Archibald, with one hand on his back
And the other clutching his huge-headed cane,
Came limping down to meet us.—"Well! well! well!"
Said he; and then he looked at my red face,
All streaked with dust and sweat, and shook my hand,
And said it must have been a right smart walk
That we had had that day from Tilbury Town.—
"Magnificent," said Isaac; and he told
About the beautiful west wind there was
Which cooled and clarified the atmosphere.
"You must have made it with your legs, I guess,"
Said Archibald; and Isaac humored him
With one of those infrequent smiles of his
Which he kept in reserve, apparently,
For Archibald alone. "But why," said he,
"Should Providence have cider in the world
If not for such an afternoon as this?"
And Archibald, with a soft light in his eyes,
Replied that if he chose to go down cellar,
There he would find eight barrels—one of which
Was newly tapped, he said, and to his taste
An honor to the fruit. Isaac approved
Most heartily of that, and guided us
Forthwith, as if his venerable feet
Were measuring the turf in his own door-yard,
Straight to the open rollway. Down we went,
Out of the fiery sunshine to the gloom,

Grateful and half sepulchral, where we found
The barrels, like eight potent sentinels,
Close ranged along the wall. From one of them
A bright pine spile stuck out alluringly,
And on the black flat stone, just under it,
Glimmered a late-spilled proof that Archibald
Had spoken from unfeigned experience.
There was a fluted antique water-glass
Close by, and in it, prisoned, or at rest,
There was a cricket, of the brown soft sort
That feeds on darkness. Isaac turned him out,
And touched him with his thumb to make him jump,
And then composedly pulled out the plug
With such a practised hand that scarce a drop
Did even touch his fingers. Then he drank
And smacked his lips with a slow patronage
And looked along the line of barrels there
With a pride that may have been forgetfulness
That they were Archibald's and not his own.
"I never twist a spigot nowadays,"
He said, and raised the glass up to the light,
"But I thank God for orchards." And that glass
Was filled repeatedly for the same hand
Before I thought it worth while to discern
Again that I was young, and that old age,
With all his woes, had some advantages.

"Now, Archibald," said Isaac, when we stood
Outside again, "I have it in my mind
That I shall take a sort of little walk—
To stretch my legs and see what you are doing.
You stay and rest your back and tell the boy
A story: Tell him all about the time
In Stafford's cabin forty years ago,

When four of us were snowed up for ten days
With only one dried haddock. Tell him all
About it, and be wary of your back.
Now I will go along."—I looked up then
At Archibald, and as I looked I saw
Just how his nostrils widened once or twice
And then grew narrow. I can hear to-day
The way the old man chuckled to himself—
Not wholesomely, not wholly to convince
Another of his mirth,—as I can hear
The lonely sigh that followed.—But at length
He said: "The orchard now's the place for us;
We may find something like an apple there,
And we shall have the shade, at any rate."
So there we went and there we laid ourselves
Where the sun could not reach us; and I champed
A dozen of worm-blighted astrakhans
While Archibald said nothing—merely told
The tale of Stafford's cabin, which was good,
Though "master chilly"—after his own phrase—
Even for a day like that. But other thoughts
Were moving in his mind, imperative,
And writhing to be spoken: I could see
The glimmer of them in a glance or two,
Cautious, or else unconscious, that he gave
Over his shoulder: . . . "Stafford and the rest—
But that's an old song now, and Archibald
And Isaac are old men. Remember, boy,
That we are old. Whatever we have gained,
Or lost, or thrown away, we are old men.
You look before you and we look behind,
And we are playing life out in the shadow—
But that's not all of it. The sunshine lights
A good road yet before us if we look,

And we are doing that when least we know it;
For both of us are children of the sun,
Like you, and like the weed there at your feet.
The shadow calls us, and it frightens us—
We think; but there's a light behind the stars
And we old fellows who have dared to live,
We see it—and we see the other things,
The other things . . . Yes, I have seen it come
These eight years, and these ten years, and I know
Now that it cannot be for very long
That Isaac will be Isaac. You have seen—
Young as you are, you must have seen the strange
Uncomfortable habit of the man?
He'll take my nerves and tie them in a knot
Sometimes, and that's not Isaac. I know that—
And I know what it is: I get it here
A little, in my knees, and Isaac—here."
The old man shook his head regretfully
And laid his knuckles three times on his forehead.
"That's what it is: Isaac is not quite right.
You see it, but you don't know what it means:
The thousand little differences—no,
You do not know them, and it's well you don't;
You'll know them soon enough—God bless you, boy!—
You'll know them, but not all of them—not all.
So think of them as little as you can:
There's nothing in them for you, or for me—
But I am old and I must think of them;
I'm in the shadow, but I don't forget
The light, my boy,—the light behind the stars.
Remember that: remember that I said it;
And when the time that you think far away
Shall come for you to say it—say it, boy;
Let there be no confusion or distrust

In you, no snarling of a life half lived,
Nor any cursing over broken things
That your complaint has been the ruin of.
Live to see clearly and the light will come
To you, and as you need it.—But there, there,
I'm going it again, as Isaac says,
And I'll stop now before you go to sleep.—
Only be sure that you growl cautiously,
And always where the shadow may not reach you."

Never shall I forget, long as I live,
The quaint thin crack in Archibald's old voice,
The lonely twinkle in his little eyes,
Or the way it made me feel to be with him.
I know I lay and looked for a long time
Down through the orchard and across the road,
Across the river and the sun-scorched hills
That ceased in a blue forest, where the world
Ceased with it. Now and then my fancy caught
A flying glimpse of a good life beyond—
Something of ships and sunlight, streets and singing,
Troy falling, and the ages coming back,
And ages coming forward: Archibald
And Isaac were good fellows in old clothes,
And Agamemnon was a friend of mine;
Ulysses coming home again to shoot
With bows and feathered arrows made another,
And all was as it should be. I was young.

So I lay dreaming of what things I would,
Calm and incorrigibly satisfied
With apples and romance and ignorance,
And the still smoke from Archibald's clay pipe.
There was a stillness over everything,
As if the spirit of heat had laid its hand

Upon the world and hushed it; and I felt
Within the mightiness of the white sun
That smote the land around us and wrought out
A fragrance from the trees, a vital warmth
And fullness for the time that was to come,
And a glory for the world beyond the forest.
The present and the future and the past,
Isaac and Archibald, the burning bush,
The Trojans and the walls of Jericho,
Were beautifully fused; and all went well
Till Archibald began to fret for Isaac
And said it was a master day for sunstroke.
That was enough to make a mummy smile,
I thought; and I remained hilarious,
In face of all precedence and respect,
Till Isaac (who had come to us unheard)
Found he had no tobacco, looked at me
Peculiarly, and asked of Archibald
What ailed the boy to make him chirrup so.
From that he told us what a blessed world
The Lord had given us.—"But, Archibald,"
He added, with a sweet severity
That made me think of peach-skins and goose-flesh,
"I'm half afraid you cut those oats of yours
A day or two before they were well set."
"They were set well enough," said Archibald,—
And I remarked the process of his nose
Before the words came out. "But never mind
Your neighbor's oats: you stay here in the shade
And rest yourself while I go find the cards.
We'll have a little game of seven-up
And let the boy keep count."—"We'll have the game,
Assuredly," said Isaac; "and I think
That I will have a drop of cider, also."

They marched away together towards the house
And left me to my childish ruminations
Upon the ways of men. I followed them
Down cellar with my fancy, and then left them
For a fairer vision of all things at once
That was anon to be destroyed again
By the sound of voices and of heavy feet—
One of the sounds of life that I remember,
Though I forget so many that rang first
As if they were thrown down to me from Sinai.

So I remember, even to this day,
Just how they sounded, how they placed themselves,
And how the game went on while I made marks
And crossed them out, and meanwhile made some Trojans.
Likewise I made Ulysses, after Isaac,
And a little after Flaxman. Archibald
Was injured when he found himself left out,
But he had no heroics, and I said so:
I told him that his white beard was too long
And too straight down to be like things in Homer.
"Quite so," said Isaac.—"Low," said Archibald;
And he threw down a deuce with a deep grin
That showed his yellow teeth and made me happy.
So they played on till a bell rang from the door,
And Archibald said, "Supper."—After that
The old men smoked while I sat watching them
And wondered with all comfort what might come
To me, and what might never come to me;
And when the time came for the long walk home
With Isaac in the twilight, I could see
The forest and the sunset and the sky-line,
No matter where it was that I was looking:

The flame beyond the boundary, the music,
The foam and the white ships, and two old men
Were things that would not leave me.—And that night
There came to me a dream—a shining one,
With two old angels in it. They had wings,
And they were sitting where a silver light
Suffused them, face to face. The wings of one
Began to palpitate as I approached,
But I was yet unseen when a dry voice
Cried thinly, with unpatronizing triumph,
"I've got you, Isaac; high, low, jack, and the game."

Isaac and Archibald have gone their way
To the silence of the loved and well-forgotten.
I knew them, and I may have laughed at them;
But there's a laughing that has honor in it,
And I have no regret for light words now.
Rather I think sometimes they may have made
Their sport of me;—but they would not do that,
They were too old for that. They were old men,
And I may laugh at them because I knew them.

AUNT IMOGEN

Aunt Imogen was coming, and therefore
The children—Jane, Sylvester, and Young George—
Were eyes and ears; for there was only one
Aunt Imogen to them in the whole world,
And she was in it only for four weeks
In fifty-two. But those great bites of time
Made all September a Queen's Festival;
And they would strive, informally, to make
The most of them.—The mother understood,
And wisely stepped away. Aunt Imogen
Was there for only one month in the year,
While she, the mother,—she was always there;
And that was what made all the difference.
She knew it must be so, for Jane had once
Expounded it to her so learnedly
That she had looked away from the child's eyes
And thought; and she had thought of many things.

There was a demonstration every time
Aunt Imogen appeared, and there was more
Than one this time. And she was at a loss
Just how to name the meaning of it all:
It puzzled her to think that she could be
So much to any crazy thing alive—
Even to her sister's little savages
Who knew no better than to be themselves;
But in the midst of her glad wonderment
She found herself besieged and overcome
By two tight arms and one tumultuous head,
And therewith half bewildered and half pained
By the joy she felt and by the sudden love
That proved itself in childhood's honest noise.

Jane, by the wings of sex, had reached her first;
And while she strangled her, approvingly,
Sylvester thumped his drum and Young George howled.
But finally, when all was rectified,
And she had stilled the clamor of Young George
By giving him a long ride on her shoulders,
They went together into the old room
That looked across the fields; and Imogen
Gazed out with a girl's gladness in her eyes,
Happy to know that she was back once more
Where there were those who knew her, and at last
Had gloriously got away again
From cabs and clattered asphalt for a while;
And there she sat and talked and looked and laughed
And made the mother and the children laugh.
Aunt Imogen made everybody laugh.

There was the feminine paradox—that she
Who had so little sunshine for herself
Should have so much for others. How it was
That she could make, and feel for making it,
So much of joy for them, and all along
Be covering, like a scar, and while she smiled,
That hungering incompleteness and regret—
That passionate ache for something of her own,
For something of herself—she never knew.
She knew that she could seem to make them all
Believe there was no other part of her
Than her persistent happiness; but the why
And how she did not know. Still none of them
Could have a thought that she was living down—
Almost as if regret were criminal,
So proud it was and yet so profitless—
The penance of a dream, and that was good.

Her sister Jane—the mother of little Jane,
Sylvester, and Young George—might make herself
Believe she knew, for she—well, she was Jane.

Young George, however, did not yield himself
To nourish the false hunger of a ghost
That made no good return. He saw too much:
The accumulated wisdom of his years
Had so conclusively made plain to him
The permanent profusion of a world
Where everybody might have everything
To do, and almost everything to eat,
That he was jubilantly satisfied
And all unthwarted by adversity.
Young George knew things. The world, he had found out,
Was a good place, and life was a good game—
Particularly when Aunt Imogen
Was in it. And one day it came to pass—
One rainy day when she was holding him
And rocking him—that he, in his own right,
Took it upon himself to tell her so;
And something in his way of telling it—
The language, or the tone, or something else—
Gripped like insidious fingers on her throat,
And then went foraging as if to make
A plaything of her heart. Such undeserved
And unsophisticated confidence
Went mercilessly home; and had she sat
Before a looking glass, the deeps of it
Could not have shown more clearly to her then
Than one thought-mirrored little glimpse had shown,
The pang that wrenched her face and filled her eyes
With anguish and intolerable mist.
The blow that she had vaguely thrust aside

Like fright so many times had found her now:
Clean-thrust and final it had come to her
From a child's lips at last, as it had come
Never before, and as it might be felt
Never again. Some grief, like some delight,
Stings hard but once: to custom after that
The rapture or the pain submits itself,
And we are wiser than we were before.
And Imogen was wiser; though at first
Her dream-defeating wisdom was indeed
A thankless heritage: there was no sweet,
No bitter now; nor was there anything
To make a daily meaning for her life—
Till truth, like Harlequin, leapt out somehow
From ambush and threw sudden savor to it—
But the blank taste of time. There were no dreams,
No phantoms in her future any more:
One clinching revelation of what was
One by-flash of irrevocable chance,
Had acridly but honestly foretold
The mystical fulfilment of a life
That might have once ... But that was all gone by:
There was no need of reaching back for that:
The triumph was not hers: there was no love
Save borrowed love: there was no might have been.

But there was yet Young George—and he had gone
Conveniently to sleep, like a good boy;
And there was yet Sylvester with his drum,
And there was frowzle-headed little Jane;
And there was Jane the sister, and the mother,—
Her sister, and the mother of them all.
They were not hers, not even one of them:
She was not born to be so much as that,

For she was born to be Aunt Imogen.
Now she could see the truth and look at it;
Now she could make stars out where once had palled
A future's emptiness; now she could share
With others—ah, the others!—to the end
The largess of a woman who could smile;
Now it was hers to dance the folly down,
And all the murmuring; now it was hers
To be Aunt Imogen.—So, when Young George
Woke up and blinked at her with his big eyes,
And smiled to see the way she blinked at him,
'T was only in old concord with the stars
That she took hold of him and held him close,
Close to herself, and crushed him till he laughed.

THE GROWTH OF "LORRAINE"

I

While I stood listening, discreetly dumb,
Lorraine was having the last word with me:
"I know," she said, "I know it, but you see
Some creatures are born fortunate, and some
Are born to be found out and overcome,—
Born to be slaves, to let the rest go free;
And if I'm one of them (and I must be)
You may as well forget me and go home.

"You tell me not to say these things, I know,
But I should never try to be content:
I've gone too far; the life would be too slow.
Some could have done it—some girls have the stuff;
But I can't do it: I don't know enough.
I'm going to the devil."—And she went.

II

I did not half believe her when she said
That I should never hear from her again;
Nor when I found a letter from Lorraine,
Was I surprised or grieved at what I read:
"Dear friend, when you find this, I shall be dead.
You are too far away to make me stop.
They say that one drop—think of it, one drop!—
Will be enough,—but I'll take five instead.

"You do not frown because I call you friend,
For I would have you glad that I still keep
Your memory, and even at the end—
Impenitent, sick, shattered—cannot curse
The love that flings, for better or for worse,
This worn-out, cast-out flesh of mine to sleep."

ERASMUS

When he protested, not too solemnly,
That for a world's achieving maintenance
The crust of overdone divinity
Lacked aliment, they called it recreance;
And when he chose through his own glass to scan
Sick Europe, and reduced, unyieldingly,
The monk within the cassock to the man
Within the monk, they called it heresy.

And when he made so perilously bold
As to be scattered forth in black and white,
Good fathers looked askance at him and rolled
Their inward eyes in anguish and affright;
There were some of them did shake at what was told
And they shook best who knew that he was right.

CORTÈGE

Four o'clock this afternoon,
Fifteen hundred miles away:
So it goes, the crazy tune,
So it pounds and hums all day.

Four o'clock this afternoon,
Earth will hide them far away:
Best they go to go so soon,
Best for them the grave to-day.

Had she gone but half so soon,
Half the world had passed away.
Four o'clock this afternoon,
Best for them they go to-day.

Four o'clock this afternoon
Love will hide them deep, they say;
Love that made the grave so soon,
Fifteen hundred miles away.

Four o'clock this afternoon—
Ah, but they go slow to-day:
Slow to suit my crazy tune,
Past the need of all we say.

Best it came to come so soon,
Best for them they go to-day:
Four o'clock this afternoon,
Fifteen hundred miles away.

VARIATIONS OF GREEK THEMES

I

A HAPPY MAN
(Carphyllides)

When these graven lines you see,
Traveler, do not pity me;
Though I be among the dead,
Let no mournful word be said.

Children that I leave behind,
And their children, all were kind;
Near to them and to my wife,
I was happy all my life.

My three sons I married right,
And their sons I rocked at night;
Death nor sorrow ever brought
Cause for one unhappy thought.

Now, and with no need of tears,
Here they leave me, full of years,—
Leave me to my quiet rest
In the region of the blest.

II

A MIGHTY RUNNER
(Nicarchus)

The day when Charmus ran with five
In Arcady, as I'm alive,
He came in seventh.—"Five and one
Make seven, you say? It can't be done."—
Well, if you think it needs a note,

A friend in a fur overcoat
Ran with him, crying all the while,
"You'll beat 'em, Charmus, by a mile!"
And so he came in seventh.
Therefore, good Zoilus, you see
The thing is plain as plain can be;
And with four more for company,
He would have been eleventh.

III
THE RAVEN
(Nicarchus)

The gloom of death is on the raven's wing.
   The song of death is in the raven's cries:
But when Demophilus begins to sing,
   The raven dies.

IV
EUTYCHIDES
(Lucilius)

Eutychides, who wrote the songs,
Is going down where he belongs.
O you unhappy ones, beware:
Eutychides will soon be there!
For he is coming with twelve lyres,
And with more than twice twelve quires
Of the stuff that he has done
In the world from which he's gone.
Ah, now must you know death indeed,
For he is coming with all speed;
And with Eutychides in Hell,
Where's a poor tortured soul to dwell?

V

DORICHA
(Posidippus)

So now the very bones of you are gone
Where they were dust and ashes long ago;
And there was the last ribbon you tied on
To bind your hair, and that is dust also;
And somewhere there is dust that was of old
A soft and scented garment that you wore—
The same that once till dawn did closely fold
You in with fair Charaxus, fair no more.

But Sappho, and the white leaves of her song,
Will make your name a word for all to learn,
And all to love thereafter, even while
It's but a name; and this will be as long
As there are distant ships that will return
Again to Naucratis and to the Nile.

VI

THE DUST OF TIMAS
(Sappho)

This dust was Timas; and they say
That almost on her wedding day
She found her bridal home to be
The dark house of Persephone.

And many maidens, knowing then
That she would not come back again,
Unbound their curls; and all in tears,
They cut them off with sharpened shears.

VII
ARETEMIAS
(Antipater of Sidon)

I'm sure I see it all now as it was,
When first you set your foot upon the shore
Where dim Cocytus flows for evermore,
And how it came to pass
That all those Dorian women who are there
In Hades, and still fair,
Came up to you, so young, and wept and smiled
When they beheld you and your little child.
And then, I'm sure, with tears upon your face
To be in that sad place,
You told of the two children you had borne,
And then of Euphron, whom you leave to mourn.
"One stays with him," you said.
"And this one I bring with me to the dead."

VIII
THE OLD STORY
(Marcus Argentarius)

Like many a one, when you had gold
Love met you smiling, we are told;
But now that all your gold is gone,
Love leaves you hungry and alone.

And women, who have called you more
Sweet names than ever were before,
Will ask another now to tell
What man you are and where you dwell.

Was ever anyone but you
So long in learning what is true?
Must you find only at the end
That who has nothing has no friend?

IX
TO-MORROW
(Macedonius)

To-morrow? Then your one word left is always now the
　　　　same;
And that's a word that names a day that has no more a name.
To-morrow, I have learned at last, is all you have to give:
The rest will be another's now, as long as I may live.
You will see me in the evening?—And what evening has
　　　　there been,
Since time began with women, but old age and wrinkled
　　　　skin?

X
LAIS TO APHRODITE
(Plato)

When I, poor Lais, with my crown
Of beauty could laugh Hellas down,
Young lovers crowded at my door,
Where now my lovers come no more.

So, Goddess, you will not refuse
A mirror that has now no use;
For what I was I cannot be,
And what I am I will not see.

XI

AN INSCRIPTION BY THE SEA
(Glaucus)

No dust have I to cover me,
    My grave no man may show;
My tomb is this unending sea,
    And I lie far below.
My fate, O stranger, was to drown;
And where it was the ship went down
    Is what the sea-birds know.

From

THE TOWN
DOWN THE RIVER

CALVERLY'S

We go no more to Calverly's,
For there the lights are few and low;
And who are there to see by them,
Or what they see, we do not know.
Poor strangers of another tongue
May now creep in from anywhere,
And we, forgotten, be no more
Than twilight on a ruin there.

We two, the remnant. All the rest
Are cold and quiet. You nor I,
Nor fiddle now, nor flagon-lid,
May ring them back from where they lie.
No fame delays oblivion
For them, but something yet survives:
A record written fair, could we
But read the book of scattered lives.

There'll be a page for Leffingwell,
And one for Lingard, the Moon-calf;
And who knows what for Clavering,
Who died because he couldn't laugh?
Who knows or cares? No sign is here,
No face, no voice, no memory;
No Lingard with his eerie joy,
No Clavering, no Calverly.

We cannot have them here with us
To say where their light lives are gone,
Or if they be of other stuff
Than are the moons of Ilion.
So, be their place of one estate
With ashes, echoes, and old wars,—
Or ever we be of the night,
Or we be lost among the stars.

MOMUS

"Where's the need of singing now?"—
Smooth your brow,
Momus, and be reconciled,
For King Kronos is a child—
Child and father,
Or god rather,
And all gods are wild.

"Who reads Byron any more?"—
Shut the door,
Momus, for I feel a draught;
Shut it quick, for some one laughed.—
"What's become of
Browning? Some of
Wordsworth lumbers like a raft?

"What are poets to find here?"—
Have no fear:
When the stars are shining blue
There will yet be left a few
Themes availing—
And these failing,
Momus, there'll be you.

THE WHITE LIGHTS

(Broadway, 1906)

When in from Delos came the gold
That held the dream of Pericles,
When first Athenian ears were told
The tumult of Euripides,
When men met Aristophanes,
Who fledged them with immortal quills—
Here, where the time knew none of these,
There were some islands and some hills.

When Rome went ravening to see
The sons of mothers end their days,
When Flaccus bade Leuconoë
To banish her Chaldean ways,
When first the pearled, alembic phrase
Of Maro into music ran—
Here there was neither blame nor praise
For Rome, or for the Mantuan.

When Avon, like a faery floor,
Lay freighted, for the eyes of One,
With galleons laden long before
By moonlit wharves in Avalon—
Here, where the white lights have begun
To seethe a way for something fair,
No prophet knew, from what was done,
That there was triumph in the air.

LEONORA

They have made for Leonora this low dwelling in the
      ground,
And with cedar they have woven the four walls round.
Like a little dryad hiding she'll be wrapped all in green,
Better kept and longer valued than by ways that would have
      been.

They will come with many roses in the early afternoon,
They will come with pinks and lilies and with Leonora soon;
And as long as beauty's garments over beauty's limbs are
      thrown,
There'll be lilies that are liars, and the rose will have its own.

There will be a wondrous quiet in the house that they have
      made,
And to-night will be a darkness in the place where she'll be
      laid;
But the builders, looking forward into time, could only see
Darker nights for Leonora than to-night shall ever be.

HOW ANNANDALE WENT OUT

"They called it Annandale—and I was there
To flourish, to find words, and to attend:
Liar, physician, hypocrite, and friend,
I watched him; and the sight was not so fair
As one or two that I have seen elsewhere:
An apparatus not for me to mend—
A wreck, with hell between him and the end,
Remained of Annandale; and I was there.

"I knew the ruin as I knew the man;
So put the two together, if you can,
Remembering the worst you know of me.
Now view yourself as I was, on the spot—
With a slight kind of engine. Do you see?
Like this . . . You wouldn't hang me? I thought not."

MINIVER CHEEVY

Miniver Cheevy, child of scorn,
    Grew lean while he assailed the seasons;
He wept that he was ever born,
    And he had reasons.

Miniver loved the days of old
    When swords were bright and steeds were prancing;
The vision of a warrior bold
    Would set him dancing.

Miniver sighed for what was not,
    And dreamed, and rested from his labors;
He dreamed of Thebes and Camelot,
    And Priam's neighbors.

Miniver mourned the ripe renown
    That made so many a name so fragrant;
He mourned Romance, now on the town,
    And Art, a vagrant.

Miniver loved the Medici,
    Albeit he had never seen one;
He would have sinned incessantly
    Could he have been one.

Miniver cursed the commonplace
    And eyed a khaki suit with loathing;
He missed the mediæval grace
    Of iron clothing.

Miniver scorned the gold he sought,
    But sore annoyed was he without it;
Miniver thought, and thought, and thought,
    And thought about it.

Miniver Cheevy, born too late,
    Scratched his head and kept on thinking;
Miniver coughed, and called it fate,
    And kept on drinking.

THE COMPANION

Let him answer as he will,
Or be lightsome as he may,
Now nor after shall he say
Worn-out words enough to kill,
Or to lull down by their craft,
Doubt, that was born yesterday,
When he lied and when she laughed.

Let him find another name
For the starlight on the snow,
Let him teach her till she know
That all seasons are the same,
And all sheltered ways are fair,—
Still, wherever she may go,
Doubt will have a dwelling there.

FOR A DEAD LADY

No more with overflowing light
Shall fill the eyes that now are faded,
Nor shall another's fringe with night
Their woman-hidden world as they did.
No more shall quiver down the days
The flowing wonder of her ways,
Whereof no language may requite
The shifting and the many-shaded.

The grace, divine, definitive,
Clings only as a faint forestalling;
The laugh that love could not forgive
Is hushed, and answers to no calling;
The forehead and the little ears
Have gone where Saturn keeps the years;
The breast where roses could not live
Has done with rising and with falling.

The beauty, shattered by the laws
That have creation in their keeping,
No longer trembles at applause,
Or over children that are sleeping;
And we who delve in beauty's lore
Know all that we have known before
Of what inexorable cause
Makes Time so vicious in his reaping.

THE REVEALER

(Roosevelt)

He turned aside to see the carcase of the lion: and behold,
there was a swarm of bees and honey in the carcase of the lion.
. . . And the men of the city said unto him, What is sweeter
than honey? and what is stronger than a lion?—*Judges,* 14.

> The palms of Mammon have disowned
> The gift of our complacency;
> The bells of ages have intoned
> Again their rhythmic irony;
> And from the shadow, suddenly,
> 'Mid echoes of decrepit rage,
> The seer of our necessity
> Confronts a Tyrian heritage.
>
> Equipped with unobscured intent
> He smiles with lions at the gate,
> Acknowledging the compliment
> Like one familiar with his fate;
> The lions, having time to wait,
> Perceive a small cloud in the skies,
> Whereon they look, disconsolate,
> With scared, reactionary eyes.
>
> A shadow falls upon the land,—
> They sniff, and they are like to roar;
> For they will never understand
> What they have never seen before.
> They march in order to the door,
> Not knowing the best thing to seek,
> Nor caring if the gods restore
> The lost composite of the Greek.

The shadow fades, the light arrives,
And ills that were concealed are seen;
The combs of long-defended hives
Now drip dishonored and unclean;
No Nazarite or Nazarene
Compels our questioning to prove
The difference that is between
Dead lions—or the sweet thereof.

But not for lions, live or dead,
Except as we are all as one,
Is he the world's accredited
Revealer of what we have done;
What You and I and Anderson
Are still to do is his reward;
If we go back when he is gone—
There is an Angel with a Sword.

He cannot close again the doors
That now are shattered for our sake;
He cannot answer for the floors
We crowd on, or for walls that shake;
He cannot wholly undertake
The cure of our immunity;
He cannot hold the stars, or make
Of seven years a century.

So Time will give us what we earn
Who flaunt the handful for the whole,
And leave us all that we may learn
Who read the surface for the soul;
And we'll be steering to the goal,

For we have said so to our sons:
When we who ride can pay the toll,
Time humors the far-seeing ones.

Down to our nose's very end
We see, and are invincible,—
Too vigilant to comprehend
The scope of what we cannot sell;
But while we seem to know as well
As we know dollars, or our skins,
The Titan may not always tell
Just where the boundary begins.

THE MAN AGAINST
THE SKY

THE GIFT OF GOD

Blessed with a joy that only she
Of all alive shall ever know,
She wears a proud humility
For what it was that willed it so,—
That her degree should be so great
Among the favored of the Lord
That she may scarcely bear the weight
Of her bewildering reward.

As one apart, immune, alone,
Or featured for the shining ones,
And like to none that she has known
Of other women's other sons,—
The firm fruition of her need,
He shines anointed; and he blurs
Her vision, till it seems indeed
A sacrilege to call him hers.

She fears a little for so much
Of what is best, and hardly dares
To think of him as one to touch
With aches, indignities, and cares;
She sees him rather at the goal,
Still shining; and her dream foretells
The proper shining of a soul
Where nothing ordinary dwells.

Perchance a canvass of the town
Would find him far from flags and shouts,
And leave him only the renown
Of many smiles and many doubts;
Perchance the crude and common tongue

Would havoc strangely with his worth;
But she, with innocence unwrung,
Would read his name around the earth.

And others, knowing how this youth
Would shine, if love could make him great,
When caught and tortured for the truth
Would only writhe and hesitate;
While she, arranging for his days
What centuries could not fulfill,
Transmutes him with her faith and praise,
And has him shining where she will.

She crowns him with her gratefulness,
And says again that life is good;
And should the gift of God be less
In him than in her motherhood,
His fame, though vague, will not be small,
As upward through her dream he fares,
Half clouded with a crimson fall
Of roses thrown on marble stairs.

JOHN GORHAM

"Tell me what you're doing over here, John Gorham,
Sighing hard and seeming to be sorry when you're not;
Make me laugh or let me go now, for long faces in the
        moonlight
Are a sign for me to say again a word that you forgot."—

"I'm over here to tell you what the moon already
May have said or maybe shouted ever since a year ago;
I'm over here to tell you what you are, Jane Wayland,
And to make you rather sorry, I should say, for being so."—

"Tell me what you're saying to me now, John Gorham,
Or you'll never see as much of me as ribbons any more;
I'll vanish in as many ways as I have toes and fingers,
And you'll not follow far for one where flocks have been
        before."—

"I'm sorry now you never saw the flocks, Jane Wayland,
But you're the one to make of them as many as you need.
And then about the vanishing. It's I who mean to vanish;
And when I'm here no longer you'll be done with me
        indeed."—

"That's a way to tell me what I am, John Gorham!
How am I to know myself until I make you smile?
Try to look as if the moon were making faces at you,
And a little more as if you meant to stay a little while."—

"You are what it is that over rose-blown gardens
Makes a pretty flutter for a season in the sun;
You are what it is that with a mouse, Jane Wayland,
Catches him and lets him go and eats him up for fun."—

"Sure I never took you for a mouse, John Gorham;
All you say is easy, but so far from being true
That I wish you wouldn't ever be again the one to think so;
For it isn't cats and butterflies that I would be to you."—

"All your little animals are in one picture—
One I've had before me since a year ago to-night;
And the picture where they live will be of you, Jane
        Wayland,
Till you find a way to kill them or to keep them out of
        sight."—

"Won't you ever see me as I am, John Gorham,
Leaving out the foolishness and all I never meant?
Somewhere in me there's a woman, if you know the way to
        find her.
Will you like me any better if I prove it and repent?"—

"I doubt if I shall ever have the time, Jane Wayland;
And I dare say all this moonlight lying round us might as
        well
Fall for nothing on the shards of broken urns that are
        forgotten,
As on two that have no longer much of anything to tell."

HILLCREST

(To Mrs. Edward MacDowell)

No sound of any storm that shakes
Old island walls with older seas
Comes here where now September makes
An island in a sea of trees.

Between the sunlight and the shade
A man may learn till he forgets
The roaring of a world remade,
And all his ruins and regrets;

And if he still remembers here
Poor fights he may have won or lost,—
If he be ridden with the fear
Of what some other fight may cost,—

If, eager to confuse too soon
What he has known with what may be,
He reads a planet out of tune
For cause of his jarred harmony,—

If here he venture to unroll
His index of adagios,
And he be given to console
Humanity with what he knows,—

He may by contemplation learn
A little more than what he knew,
And even see great oaks return
To acorns out of which they grew.

He may, if he but listen well,
Through twilight and the silence here,
Be told what there are none may tell
To vanity's impatient ear;

And he may never dare again
Say what awaits him, or be sure
What sunlit labyrinth of pain
He may not enter and endure.

Who knows to-day from yesterday
May learn to count no thing too strange:
Love builds of what Time takes away,
Till Death itself is less than Change.

Who sees enough in his duress
May go as far as dreams have gone;
Who sees a little may do less
Than many who are blind have done;

Who sees unchastened here the soul
Triumphant has no other sight
Than has a child who sees the whole
World radiant with his own delight.

Far journeys and hard wandering
Await him in whose crude surmise
Peace, like a mask, hides everything
That is and has been from his eyes;

And all his wisdom is unfound,
Or like a web that error weaves
On airy looms that have a sound
No louder now than falling leaves.

BEN JONSON ENTERTAINS
A MAN FROM STRATFORD

You are a friend then, as I make it out,
Of our man Shakespeare, who alone of us
Will put an ass's head in Fairyland
As he would add a shilling to more shillings,
All most harmonious,—and out of his
Miraculous inviolable increase
Fills Ilion, Rome, or any town you like
Of olden time with timeless Englishmen;
And I must wonder what you think of him—
All you down there where your small Avon flows
By Stratford, and where you're an Alderman.
Some, for a guess, would have him riding back
To be a farrier there, or say a dyer;
Or maybe one of your adept surveyors;
Or like enough the wizard of all tanners.
Not you—no fear of that; for I discern
In you a kindling of the flame that saves—
The nimble element, the true caloric;
I see it, and was told of it, moreover,
By our discriminate friend himself, no other.
Had you been one of the sad average,
As he would have it,—meaning, as I take it,
The sinew and the solvent of our Island,
You'd not be buying beer for this Terpander's
Approved and estimated friend Ben Jonson;
He'd never foist it as a part of his
Contingent entertainment of a townsman
While he goes off rehearsing, as he must,
If he shall ever be the Duke of Stratford.
And my words are no shadow on your town—
Far from it; for one town's as like another

As all are unlike London. Oh, he knows it,—
And there's the Stratford in him; he denies it,
And there's the Shakespeare in him. So, God help him!
I tell him he needs Greek; but neither God
Nor Greek will help him. Nothing will help that man.
You see the fates have given him so much,
He must have all or perish,—or look out
Of London, where he sees too many lords.
They're part of half what ails him: I suppose
There's nothing fouler down among the demons
Than what it is he feels when he remembers
The dust and sweat and ointment of his calling
With his lords looking on and laughing at him.
King as he is, he can't be king *de facto,*
And that's as well, because he wouldn't like it;
He'd frame a lower rating of men then
Than he has now; and after that would come
An abdication or an apoplexy.
He can't be king, not even king of Stratford,—
Though half the world, if not the whole of it,
May crown him with a crown that fits no king
Save Lord Apollo's homesick emissary:
Not there on Avon, or on any stream
Where Naiads and their white arms are no more,
Shall he find home again. It's all too bad.
But there's a comfort, for he'll have that House—
The best you ever saw; and he'll be there
Anon, as you're an Alderman. Good God!
He makes me lie awake o'nights and laugh.

And you have known him from his origin,
You tell me; and a most uncommon urchin
He must have been to the few seeing ones—
A trifle terrifying, I dare say,

Discovering a world with his man's eyes,
Quite as another lad might see some finches,
If he looked hard and had an eye for nature.
But this one had his eyes and their foretelling,
And he had you to fare with, and what else?
He must have had a father and a mother—
In fact I've heard him say so—and a dog,
As a boy should, I venture; and the dog,
Most likely, was the only man who knew him.
A dog, for all I know, is what he needs
As much as anything right here to-day,
To counsel him about his disillusions,
Old aches, and parturitions of what's coming,—
A dog of orders, an emeritus,
To wag his tail at him when he comes home,
And then to put his paws up on his knees
And say, "For God's sake, what's it all about?"

I don't know whether he needs a dog or not—
Or what he needs. I tell him he needs Greek;
I'll talk of rules and Aristotle with him,
And if his tongue's at home he'll say to that,
"I have your word that Aristotle knows,
And you mine that I don't know Aristotle."
He's all at odds with all the unities,
And what's yet worse, it doesn't seem to matter;
He treads along through Time's old wilderness
As if the tramp of all the centuries
Had left no roads—and there are none, for him;
He doesn't see them, even with those eyes,—
And that's a pity, or I say it is.
Accordingly we have him as we have him—
Going his way, the way that he goes best,
A pleasant animal with no great noise

Or nonsense anywhere to set him off—
Save only divers and inclement devils
Have made of late his heart their dwelling place.
A flame half ready to fly out sometimes
At some annoyance may be fanned up in him,
But soon it falls, and when it falls goes out;
He knows how little room there is in there
For crude and futile animosities,
And how much for the joy of being whole,
And how much for long sorrow and old pain.
On our side there are some who may be given
To grow old wondering what he thinks of us
And some above us, who are, in his eyes,
Above himself,—and that's quite right and English.
Yet here we smile, or disappoint the gods
Who made it so: the gods have always eyes
To see men scratch; and they see one down here
Who itches, manor-bitten to the bone,
Albeit he knows himself—yes, yes, he knows—
The lord of more than England and of more
Than all the seas of England in all time
Shall ever wash. D'ye wonder that I laugh?
He sees me, and he doesn't seem to care;
And why the devil should he? I can't tell you.

I'll meet him out alone of a bright Sunday,
Trim, rather spruce, and quite the gentleman.
"What ho, my lord!" say I. He doesn't hear me;
Wherefore I have to pause and look at him.
He's not enormous, but one looks at him.
A little on the round if you insist,
For now, God save the mark, he's growing old;
He's five and forty, and to hear him talk
These days you'd call him eighty; then you'd add

More years to that. He's old enough to be
The father of a world, and so he is.
"Ben, you're a scholar, what's the time of day?"
Says he; and there shines out of him again
An aged light that has no age or station—
The mystery that's his—a mischievous
Half-mad serenity that laughs at fame
For being won so easy, and at friends
Who laugh at him for what he wants the most,
And for his dukedom down in Warwickshire;—
By which you see we're all a little jealous. . . .
Poor Greene! I fear the color of his name
Was even as that of his ascending soul;
And he was one where there are many others,—
Some scrivening to the end against their fate,
Their puppets all in ink and all to die there;
And some with hands that once would shade an eye
That scanned Euripides and Æschylus
Will reach by this time for a pot-house mop
To slush their first and last of royalties.
Poor devils! and they all play to his hand;
For so it was in Athens and old Rome.
But that's not here or there; I've wandered off.
Greene does it, or I'm careful. Where's that boy?

Yes, he'll go back to Stratford. And we'll miss him?
Dear sir, there'll be no London here without him.
We'll all be riding, one of these fine days,
Down there to see him—and his wife won't like us;
And then we'll think of what he never said
Of women—which, if taken all in all
With what he did say, would buy many horses.
Though nowadays he's not so much for women:
"So few of them," he says, "are worth the guessing."

But there's a worm at work when he says that,
And while he says it one feels in the air
A deal of circumambient hocus-pocus.
They've had him dancing till his toes were tender,
And he can feel 'em now, come chilly rains.
There's no long cry for going into it,
However, and we don't know much about it.
But you in Stratford, like most here in London,
Have more now in the *Sonnets* than you paid for;
He's put one there with all her poison on,
To make a singing fiction of a shadow
That's in his life a fact, and always will be.
But she's no care of ours, though Time, I fear,
Will have a more reverberant ado
About her than about another one
Who seems to have decoyed him, married him,
And sent him scuttling on his way to London,—
With much already learned, and more to learn,
And more to follow. Lord! how I see him now,
Pretending, maybe trying, to be like us.
Whatever he may have meant, we never had him;
He failed us, or escaped, or what you will,—
And there was that about him (God knows what,—
We'd flayed another had he tried it on us)
That made as many of us as had wits
More fond of all his easy distances
Than one another's noise and clap-your-shoulder.
But think you not, my friend, he'd never talk!
Talk? He was eldritch at it; and we listened—
Thereby acquiring much we knew before
About ourselves, and hitherto had held
Irrelevant, or not prime to the purpose.
And there were some, of course, and there be now,
Disordered and reduced amazedly

To resignation by the mystic seal
Of young finality the gods had laid
On everything that made him a young demon;
And one or two shot looks at him already
As he had been their executioner;
And once or twice he was, not knowing it,—
Or knowing, being sorry for poor clay
And saying nothing. . . . Yet, for all his engines,
You'll meet a thousand of an afternoon
Who strut and sun themselves and see around 'em
A world made out of more that has a reason
Than his, I swear, that he sees here to-day;
Though he may scarcely give a Fool an exit
But we mark how he sees in everything
A law that, given we flout it once too often,
Brings fire and iron down on our naked heads.
To me it looks as if the power that made him,
For fear of giving all things to one creature,
Left out the first,—faith, innocence, illusion,
Whatever 'tis that keeps us out o' Bedlam,—
And thereby, for his too consuming vision,
Empowered him out of nature; though to see him,
You'd never guess what's going on inside him.
He'll break out some day like a keg of ale
With too much independent frenzy in it;
And all for cellaring what he knows won't keep,
And what he'd best forget—but that he can't.
You'll have it, and have more than I'm foretelling;
And there'll be such a roaring at the Globe
As never stunned the bleeding gladiators.
He'll have to change the color of its hair
A bit, for now he calls it Cleopatra.
Black hair would never do for Cleopatra.

But you and I are not yet two old women,
And you're a man of office. What he does
Is more to you than how it is he does it,—
And that's what the Lord God has never told him.
They work together, and the Devil helps 'em;
They do it of a morning, or if not,
They do it of a night; in which event
He's peevish of a morning. He seems old;
He's not the proper stomach or the sleep—
And they're two sovran agents to conserve him
Against the fiery art that has no mercy
But what's in that prodigious grand new House.
I gather something happening in his boyhood
Fulfilled him with a boy's determination
To make all Stratford 'ware of him. Well, well,
I hope at last he'll have his joy of it,
And all his pigs and sheep and bellowing beeves,
And frogs and owls and unicorns, moreover,
Be less than hell to his attendant ears.
Oh, past a doubt we'll all go down to see him.

He may be wise. With London two days off,
Down there some wind of heaven may yet revive him:
But there's no quickening breath from anywhere
Shall make of him again the poised young faun
From Warwickshire, who'd made, it seems, already
A legend of himself before I came
To blink before the last of his first lightning.
Whatever there be, there'll be no more of that;
The coming on of his old monster Time
Has made him a still man; and he has dreams
Were fair to think on once, and all found hollow.

He knows how much of what men paint themselves
Would blister in the light of what they are;
He sees how much of what was great now shares
An eminence transformed and ordinary;
He knows too much of what the world has hushed
In others, to be loud now for himself;
He knows now at what height low enemies
May reach his heart, and high friends let him fall;
But what not even such as he may know
Bedevils him the worst: his lark may sing
At heaven's gate how he will, and for as long
As joy may listen, but *he* sees no gate,
Save one whereat the spent clay waits a little
Before the churchyard has it, and the worm.
Not long ago, late in an afternoon,
I came on him unseen down Lambeth way,
And on my life I was afear'd of him:
He gloomed and mumbled like a soul from Tophet,
His hands behind him and his head bent solemn.
"What is it now," said I,—"another woman?"
That made him sorry for me, and he smiled.
"No, Ben," he mused; "it's Nothing. It's all Nothing.
We come, we go; and when we're done, we're done.
Spiders and flies—we're mostly one or t'other—
We come, we go; and when we're done, we're done."
"By God, you sing that song as if you knew it!"
Said I, by way of cheering him; "what ails ye?"
"I think I must have come down here to think,"
Says he to that, and pulls his little beard;
"Your fly will serve as well as anybody,
And what's his hour? He flies, and flies, and flies,
And in his fly's mind has a brave appearance;
And then your spider gets him in her net,

And eats him out, and hangs him up to dry.
That's Nature, the kind mother of us all.
And then your slattern housemaid swings her broom,
And where's your spider? And that's Nature, also.
It's Nature, and it's Nothing. It's all Nothing.
It's all a world where bugs and emperors
Go singularly back to the same dust,
Each in his time; and the old, ordered stars
That sang together, Ben, will sing the same
Old stave to-morrow."

                  When he talks like that,
There's nothing for a human man to do
But lead him to some grateful nook like this
Where we be now, and there to make him drink.
He'll drink, for love of me, and then be sick;
A sad sign always in a man of parts,
And always very ominous. The great
Should be as large in liquor as in love,—
And our great friend is not so large in either:
One disaffects him, and the other fails him;
Whatso he drinks that has an antic in it,
He's wondering what's to pay in his insides;
And while his eyes are on the Cyprian
He's fribbling all the time with that damned House.
We laugh here at his thrift, but after all
It may be thrift that saves him from the devil;
God gave it, anyhow,—and we'll suppose
He knew the compound of his handiwork.
To-day the clouds are with him, but anon
He'll out of 'em enough to shake the tree
Of life itself and bring down fruit unheard-of,—
And, throwing in the bruised and whole together,
Prepare a wine to make us drunk with wonder;

And if he live, there'll be a sunset spell
Thrown over him as over a glassed lake
That yesterday was all a black wild water.

God send he live to give us, if no more,
What now's a-rampage in him, and exhibit,
With a decent half-allegiance to the ages
An earnest of at least a casual eye
Turned once on what he owes to Gutenberg,
And to the fealty of more centuries
Than are as yet a picture in our vision.
"There's time enough,—I'll do it when I'm old,
And we're immortal men," he says to that;
And then he says to me, "Ben, what's 'immortal'?
Think you by any force of ordination
It may be nothing of a sort more noisy
Than a small oblivion of component ashes
That of a dream-addicted world was once
A moving atomy much like your friend here?"
Nothing will help that man. To make him laugh,
I said then he was a mad mountebank,—
And by the Lord I nearer made him cry.
I could have eat an eft then, on my knees,
Tail, claws, and all of him; for I had stung
The king of men, who had no sting for me,
And I had hurt him in his memories;
And I say now, as I shall say again,
I love the man this side idolatry.

He'll do it when he's old, he says. I wonder.
He may not be so ancient as all that.
For such as he, the thing that is to do
Will do itself,—but there's a reckoning;
The sessions that are now too much his own,
The roiling inward of a stilled outside,

The churning out of all those blood-fed lines,
The nights of many schemes and little sleep,
The full brain hammered hot with too much thinking,
The vexed heart over-worn with too much aching,—
This weary jangling of conjoined affairs
Made out of elements that have no end,
And all confused at once, I understand,
Is not what makes a man to live forever.
O no, not now! He'll not be going now:
There'll be time yet for God knows what explosions
Before he goes. He'll stay awhile. Just wait:
Just wait a year or two for Cleopatra,
For she's to be a balsam and a comfort;
And that's not all a jape of mine now, either.
For granted once the old way of Apollo
Sings in a man, he may then, if he's able,
Strike unafraid whatever strings he will
Upon the last and wildest of new lyres;
Nor out of his new magic, though it hymn
The shrieks of dungeoned hell, shall he create
A madness or a gloom to shut quite out
A cleaving daylight, and a last great calm
Triumphant over shipwreck and all storms.
He might have given Aristotle creeps,
But surely would have given him his *katharsis*.

He'll not be going yet. There's too much yet
Unsung within the man. But when he goes,
I'd stake ye coin o' the realm his only care
For a phantom world he sounded and found wanting
Will be a portion here, a portion there,
Of this or that thing or some other thing
That has a patent and intrinsical
Equivalence in those egregious shillings.

And yet he knows, God help him! Tell me, now,
If ever there was anything let loose
On earth by gods or devils heretofore
Like this mad, careful, proud, indifferent Shakespeare!
Where was it, if it ever was? By heaven,
'Twas never yet in Rhodes or Pergamon—
In Thebes or Nineveh, a thing like this!
No thing like this was ever out of England;
And that he knows. I wonder if he cares.
Perhaps he does. . . . O Lord, that House in Stratford!

EROS TURANNOS

She fears him, and will always ask
   What fated her to choose him;
She meets in his engaging mask
   All reasons to refuse him;
But what she meets and what she fears
Are less than are the downward years,
Drawn slowly to the foamless weirs
   Of age, were she to lose him.

Between a blurred sagacity
   That once had power to sound him,
And Love, that will not let him be
   The Judas that she found him,
Her pride assuages her almost,
As if it were alone the cost.—
He sees that he will not be lost,
   And waits and looks around him.

A sense of ocean and old trees
   Envelops and allures him;
Tradition, touching all he sees,
   Beguiles and reassures him;
And all her doubts of what he says
Are dimmed with what she knows of days—
Till even prejudice delays
   And fades, and she secures him.

The falling leaf inaugurates
   The reign of her confusion;
The pounding wave reverberates
   The dirge of her illusion;
And home, where passion lived and died,

Becomes a place where she can hide,
While all the town and harbor side
   Vibrate with her seclusion.

We tell you, tapping on our brows,
   The story as it should be,—
As if the story of a house
   Were told, or ever could be;
We'll have no kindly veil between
Her visions and those we have seen,—
As if we guessed what hers have been,
   Or what they are or would be.

Meanwhile we do no harm; for they
   That with a god have striven,
Not hearing much of what we say,
   Take what the god has given;
Though like waves breaking it may be,
Or like a changed familiar tree,
Or like a stairway to the sea
   Where down the blind are driven.

OLD TRAILS

(Washington Square)

I met him, as one meets a ghost or two,
Between the gray Arch and the old Hotel.
"King Solomon was right, there's nothing new,"
Said he. "Behold a ruin who meant well."

He led me down familiar steps again,
Appealingly, and set me in a chair.
"My dreams have all come true to other men,"
Said he; "God lives, however, and why care?

"An hour among the ghosts will do no harm."
He laughed, and something glad within me sank.
I may have eyed him with a faint alarm,
For now his laugh was lost in what he drank.

"They chill things here with ice from hell," he said;
"I might have known it." And he made a face
That showed again how much of him was dead,
And how much was alive and out of place,

And out of reach. He knew as well as I
That all the words of wise men who are skilled
In using them are not much to defy
What comes when memory meets the unfulfilled.

What evil and infirm perversity
Had been at work with him to bring him back?
Never among the ghosts, assuredly,
Would he originate a new attack;

Never among the ghosts, or anywhere,
Till what was dead of him was put away,
Would he attain to his offended share
Of honor among others of his day.

"You ponder like an owl," he said at last;
"You always did, and here you have a cause.
For I'm a confirmation of the past,
A vengeance, and a flowering of what was.

"Sorry? Of course you are, though you compress,
With even your most impenetrable fears,
A placid and a proper consciousness
Of anxious angels over my arrears.

"I see them there against me in a book
As large as hope, in ink that shines by night.
Surely I see; but now I'd rather look
At you, and you are not a pleasant sight.

"Forbear, forgive. Ten years are on my soul,
And on my conscience. I've an incubus:
My one distinction, and a parlous toll
To glory; but hope lives on clamorous.

" 'Twas hope, though heaven I grant you knows of what—
The kind that blinks and rises when it falls,
Whether it sees a reason why or not—
That heard Broadway's hard-throated siren-calls;

" 'Twas hope that brought me through December storms,
To shores again where I'll not have to be
A lonely man with only foreign worms
To cheer him in his last obscurity.

"But what it was that hurried me down here
To be among the ghosts, I leave to you.
My thanks are yours, no less, for one thing clear:
Though you are silent, what you say is true.

"There may have been the devil in my feet,
For down I blundered, like a fugitive,
To find the old room in Eleventh Street.
God save us!—I came here again to live."

We rose at that, and all the ghosts rose then,
And followed us unseen to his old room.
No longer a good place for living men
We found it, and we shivered in the gloom.

The goods he took away from there were few,
And soon we found ourselves outside once more,
Where now the lamps along the Avenue
Bloomed white for miles above an iron floor.

"Now lead me to the newest of hotels,"
He said, "and let your spleen be undeceived:
This ruin is not myself, but some one else;
I haven't failed; I've merely not achieved."

Whether he knew or not, he laughed and dined
With more of an immune regardlessness
Of pits before him and of sands behind
Than many a child at forty would confess;

And after, when the bells in *Boris* rang
Their tumult at the Metropolitan,
He rocked himself, and I believe he sang.
"God lives," he crooned aloud, "and I'm the man!"

He was. And even though the creature spoiled
All prophecies, I cherish his acclaim.
Three weeks he fattened; and five years he toiled
In Yonkers,—and then sauntered into fame.

And he may go now to what streets he will—
Eleventh, or the last, and little care;
But he would find the old room very still
Of evenings, and the ghosts would all be there.

I doubt if he goes after them; I doubt
If many of them ever come to him.
His memories are like lamps, and they go out;
Or if they burn, they flicker and are dim.

A light of other gleams he has to-day
And adulations of applauding hosts;
A famous danger, but a safer way
Than growing old alone among the ghosts.

But we may still be glad that we were wrong:
He fooled us, and we'd shrivel to deny it;
Though sometimes when old echoes ring too long,
I wish the bells in *Boris* would be quiet.

THE UNFORGIVEN

When he, who is the unforgiven,
Beheld her first, he found her fair:
No promise ever dreamt in heaven
Could then have lured him anywhere
That would have been away from there;
And all his wits had lightly striven,
Foiled with her voice, and eyes, and hair.

There's nothing in the saints and sages
To meet the shafts her glances had,
Or such as hers have had for ages
To blind a man till he be glad,
And humble him till he be mad.
The story would have many pages,
And would be neither good nor bad.

And, having followed, you would find him
Where properly the play begins;
But look for no red light behind him—
No fumes of many-colored sins,
Fanned high by screaming violins.
God knows what good it was to blind him,
Or whether man or woman wins.

And by the same eternal token,
Who knows just how it will all end?—
This drama of hard words unspoken,
This fireside farce, without a friend
Or enemy to comprehend
What augurs when two lives are broken,
And fear finds nothing left to mend.

He stares in vain for what awaits him,
And sees in Love a coin to toss;
He smiles, and her cold hush berates him

Beneath his hard half of the cross;
They wonder why it ever was;
And she, the unforgiving, hates him
More for her lack than for her loss.

He feeds with pride his indecision,
And shrinks from what will not occur,
Bequeathing with infirm derision
His ashes to the days that were,
Before she made him prisoner;
And labors to retrieve the vision
That he must once have had of her.

He waits, and there awaits an ending,
And he knows neither what nor when;
But no magicians are attending
To make him see as he saw then,
And he will never find again
The face that once had been the rending
Of all his purpose among men.

He blames her not, nor does he chide her,
And she has nothing new to say;
If he were Bluebeard he could hide her,
But that's not written in the play,
And there will be no change to-day;
Although, to the serene outsider,
There still would seem to be a way.

VETERAN SIRENS

The ghost of Ninon would be sorry now
To laugh at them, were she to see them here,
So brave and so alert for learning how
To fence with reason for another year.

Age offers a far comelier diadem
Than theirs; but anguish has no eye for grace,
When time's malicious mercy cautions them
To think a while of number and of space.

The burning hope, the worn expectancy,
The martyred humor, and the maimed allure,
Cry out for time to end his levity,
And age to soften its investiture;

But they, though others fade and are still fair,
Defy their fairness and are unsubdued;
Although they suffer, they may not forswear
The patient ardor of the unpursued.

Poor flesh, to fight the calendar so long;
Poor vanity, so quaint and yet so brave;
Poor folly, so deceived and yet so strong,
So far from Ninon and so near the grave.

ANOTHER DARK LADY

Think not, because I wonder where you fled,
That I would lift a pin to see you there;
You may, for me, be prowling anywhere,
So long as you show not your little head:
No dark and evil story of the dead
Would leave you less pernicious or less fair—
Not even Lilith, with her famous hair;
And Lilith was the devil, I have read.

I cannot hate you, for I loved you then.
The woods were golden then. There was a road
Through beeches; and I said their smooth feet showed
Like yours. Truth must have heard me from afar,
For I shall never have to learn again
That yours are cloven as no beech's are.

The Poor Relation

No longer torn by what she knows
And sees within the eyes of others,
Her doubts are when the daylight goes,
Her fears are for the few she bothers.
She tells them it is wholly wrong
Of her to stay alive so long;
And when she smiles her forehead shows
A crinkle that had been her mother's.

Beneath her beauty, blanched with pain,
And wistful yet for being cheated,
A child would seem to ask again
A question many times repeated;
But no rebellion has betrayed
Her wonder at what she has paid
For memories that have no stain,
For triumph born to be defeated.

To those who come for what she was—
The few left who know where to find her—
She clings, for they are all she has;
And she may smile when they remind her,
As heretofore, of what they know
Of roses that are still to blow
By ways where not so much as grass
Remains of what she sees behind her.

They stay a while, and having done
What penance or the past requires,
They go, and leave her there alone
To count her chimneys and her spires.
Her lip shakes when they go away,

And yet she would not have them stay;
She knows as well as anyone
That Pity, having played, soon tires.

But one friend always reappears,
A good ghost, not to be forsaken;
Whereat she laughs and has no fears
Of what a ghost may reawaken,
But welcomes, while she wears and mends
The poor relation's odds and ends,
Her truant from a tomb of years—
Her power of youth so early taken.

Poor laugh, more slender than her song
It seems; and there are none to hear it
With even the stopped ears of the strong
For breaking heart or broken spirit.
The friends who clamored for her place,
And would have scratched her for her face,
Have lost her laughter for so long
That none would care enough to fear it.

None live who need fear anything
From her, whose losses are their pleasure;
The plover with a wounded wing
Stays not the flight that others measure;
So there she waits, and while she lives,
And death forgets, and faith forgives,
Her memories go foraging
For bits of childhood song they treasure.

And like a giant harp that hums
On always, and is always blending
The coming of what never comes
With what has past and had an ending,

The City trembles, throbs, and pounds
Outside, and through a thousand sounds
The small intolerable drums
Of Time are like slow drops descending.

Bereft enough to shame a sage
And given little to long sighing,
With no illusion to assuage
The lonely changelessness of dying,—
Unsought, unthought-of, and unheard,
She sings and watches like a bird,
Safe in a comfortable cage
From which there will be no more flying.

BEWICK FINZER

Time was when his half million drew
    The breath of six per cent;
But soon the worm of what-was-not
    Fed hard on his content;
And something crumbled in his brain
    When his half million went.

Time passed, and filled along with his
    The place of many more;
Time came, and hardly one of us
    Had credence to restore,
From what appeared one day, the man
    Whom we had known before.

The broken voice, the withered neck,
    The coat worn out with care,
The cleanliness of indigence,
    The brilliance of despair,
The fond imponderable dreams
    Of affluence,—all were there.

Poor Finzer, with his dreams and schemes,
    Fares hard now in the race,
With heart and eye that have a task
    When he looks in the face
Of one who might so easily
    Have been in Finzer's place.

He comes unfailing for the loan
    We give and then forget;
He comes, and probably for years
    Will he be coming yet,—
Familiar as an old mistake,
    And futile as regret.

BOKARDO

Well, Bokardo, here we are;
    Make yourself at home.
Look around—you haven't far
    To look—and why be dumb?
Not the place that used to be,
Not so many things to see;
But there's room for you and me.
    And you—you've come.

Talk a little; or, if not,
    Show me with a sign
Why it was that you forgot
    What was yours and mine.
Friends, I gather, are small things
In an age when coins are kings;
Even at that, one hardly flings
    Friends before swine.

Rather strong? I knew as much,
    For it made you speak.
No offense to swine, as such,
    But why this hide-and-seek?
You have something on your side,
And you wish you might have died,
So you tell me. And you tried
    One night last week?

You tried hard? And even then
    Found a time to pause?
When you try as hard again,
    You'll have another cause.
When you find yourself at odds

With all dreamers of all gods,
You may smite yourself with rods—
    But not the laws.

Though they seem to show a spite
    Rather devilish,
They move on as with a might
    Stronger than your wish.
Still, however strong they be,
They bide man's authority:
Xerxes, when he flogged the sea,
    May've scared a fish.

It's a comfort, if you like,
    To keep honor warm,
But as often as you strike
    The laws, you do no harm.
To the laws, I mean. To you—
That's another point of view,
One you may as well indue
    With some alarm.

Not the most heroic face
    To present, I grant;
Nor will you insure disgrace
    By fearing what you want.
Freedom has a world of sides,
And if reason once derides
Courage, then your courage hides
    A deal of cant.

Learn a little to forget
    Life was once a feast;
You aren't fit for dying yet,
    So don't be a beast.

Few men with a mind will say,
Thinking twice, that they can pay
Half their debts of yesterday,
        Or be released.

There's a debt now on your mind
        More than any gold?
And there's nothing you can find
        Out there in the cold?
Only—what's his name?—Remorse?
And Death riding on his horse?
Well, be glad there's nothing worse
        Than you have told.

Leave Remorse to warm his hands
        Outside in the rain.
As for Death, he understands,
        And he will come again.
Therefore, till your wits are clear,
Flourish and be quiet—here.
But a devil at each ear
        Will be a strain?

Past a doubt they will indeed,
        More than you have earned.
I say that because you need
        Ablution, being burned?
Well, if you must have it so,
Your last flight went rather low.
Better say you had to know
        What you have learned.

And that's over. Here you are,
        Battered by the past.
Time will have his little scar,
        But the wound won't last.

Nor shall harrowing surprise
Find a world without its eyes
If a star fades when the skies
    Are overcast.

God knows there are lives enough,
    Crushed, and too far gone
Longer to make sermons of,
    And those we leave alone.
Others, if they will, may rend
The worn patience of a friend
Who, though smiling, sees the end,
    With nothing done.

But your fervor to be free
    Fled the faith it scorned;
Death demands a decency
    Of you, and you are warned.
But for all we give we get
Mostly blows? Don't be upset;
You, Bokardo, are not yet
    Consumed or mourned.

There'll be falling into view
    Much to rearrange;
And there'll be a time for you
    To marvel at the change.
They that have the least to fear
Question hardest what is here;
When long-hidden skies are clear,
    The stars look strange.

THE THREE TAVERNS

THE VALLEY OF THE SHADOW

There were faces to remember in the Valley of the
       Shadow,
There were faces unregarded, there were faces to forget;
There were fires of grief and fear that are a few forgotten
       ashes,
There were sparks of recognition that are not forgotten
       yet.
For at first, with an amazed and overwhelming
       indignation
At a measureless malfeasance that obscurely willed it
       thus,
They were lost and unacquainted—till they found
       themselves in others,
Who had groped as they were groping where dim ways were
       perilous.

There were lives that were as dark as are the fears and
       intuitions
Of a child who knows himself and is alone with what he
       knows;
There were pensioners of dreams and there were debtors of
       illusions,
All to fail before the triumph of a weed that only grows.
There were thirsting heirs of golden sieves that held not
       wine or water,
And had no names in traffic or more value there than toys:
There were blighted sons of wonder in the Valley of the
       Shadow,
Where they suffered and still wondered why their wonder
       made no noise.

There were slaves who dragged the shackles of a precedent
      unbroken,
Demonstrating the fulfilment of unalterable schemes,
Which had been, before the cradle, Time's inexorable
      tenants
Of what were now the dusty ruins of their father's dreams.
There were these, and there were many who had stumbled
      up to manhood,
Where they saw too late the road they should have taken
      long ago:
There were thwarted clerks and fiddlers in the Valley of the
      Shadow,
The commemorative wreckage of what others did not
      know.

And there were daughters older than the mothers who had
      borne them,
Being older in their wisdom, which is older than the earth;
And they were going forward only farther into darkness,
Unrelieved as were the blasting obligations of their
      birth;
And among them, giving always what was not for their
      possession,
There were maidens, very quiet, with no quiet in their
      eyes;
There were daughters of the silence in the Valley of the
      Shadow,
Each an isolated item in the family sacrifice.

There were creepers among catacombs where dull regrets
      were torches,
Giving light enough to show them what was there upon the
      shelves—
Where there was more for them to see than pleasure would
      remember
Of something that had been alive and once had been
      themselves.
There were some who stirred the ruins with a solid
      imprecation,
While as many fled repentance for the promise of despair:
There were drinkers of wrong waters in the Valley of the
      Shadow,
And all the sparkling ways were dust that once had led them
      there.

There were some who knew the steps of Age incredibly
      beside them,
And his fingers upon shoulders that had never felt the
      wheel;
And their last of empty trophies was a gilded cup of
      nothing,
Which a contemplating vagabond would not have come to
      steal.
Long and often had they figured for a larger valuation,
But the size of their addition was the balance of a doubt:
There were gentlemen of leisure in the Valley of the
      Shadow,
Not allured by retrospection, disenchanted, and played
      out.

And among the dark endurances of unavowed reprisals
There were silent eyes of envy that saw little but saw well;
And over beauty's aftermath of hazardous ambitions
There were tears for what had vanished as they vanished
     where they fell.
Not assured of what was theirs, and always hungry for the
     nameless,
There were some whose only passion was for Time who
     made them cold:
There were numerous fair women in the Valley of the
     Shadow,
Dreaming rather less of heaven than of hell when they were
     old.

Now and then, as if to scorn the common touch of common
     sorrow,
There were some who gave a few the distant pity of a smile;
And another cloaked a soul as with an ash of human embers,
Having covered thus a treasure that would last him for a
     while.
There were many by the presence of the many disaffected,
Whose exemption was included in the weight that others
     bore:
There were seekers after darkness in the Valley of the
     Shadow,
And they alone were there to find what they were looking
     for.

So they were, and so they are; and as they came are coming
     others,
And among them are the fearless and the meek and the
     unborn;

And a question that has held us heretofore without an
        answer
May abide without an answer until all have ceased to mourn.
For the children of the dark are more to name than are the
        wretched,
Or the broken, or the weary, or the baffled, or the shamed:
There are builders of new mansions in the Valley of the
        Shadow,
And among them are the dying and the blinded and the
        maimed.

THE WANDERING JEW

I saw by looking in his eyes
That they remembered everything;
And this was how I came to know
That he was here, still wandering.
For though the figure and the scene
Were never to be reconciled,
I knew the man as I had known
His image when I was a child.

With evidence at every turn,
I should have held it safe to guess
That all the newness of New York
Had nothing new in loneliness;
Yet here was one who might be Noah,
Or Nathan, or Abimelech,
Or Lamech, out of ages lost,—
Or, more than all, Melchizedek.

Assured that he was none of these,
I gave them back their names again,
To scan once more those endless eyes
Where all my questions ended then.
I found in them what they revealed
That I shall not live to forget,
And wondered if they found in mine
Compassion that I might regret.

Pity, I learned, was not the least
Of time's offending benefits
That had now for so long impugned
The conservation of his wits:
Rather it was that I should yield,

Alone, the fealty that presents
The tribute of a tempered ear
To an untempered eloquence.

Before I pondered long enough
On whence he came and who he was,
I trembled at his ringing wealth
Of manifold anathemas;
I wondered, while he seared the world,
What new defection ailed the race,
And if it mattered how remote
Our fathers were from such a place.

Before there was an hour for me
To contemplate with less concern
The crumbling realm awaiting us
Than his that was beyond return,
A dawning on the dust of years
Had shaped with an elusive light
Mirages of remembered scenes
That were no longer for the sight.

For now the gloom that hid the man
Became a daylight on his wrath,
And one wherein my fancy viewed
New lions ramping in his path.
The old were dead and had no fangs,
Wherefore he loved them—seeing not
They were the same that in their time
Had eaten everything they caught.

The world around him was a gift
Of anguish to his eyes and ears,
And one that he had long reviled
As fit for devils, not for seers.

Where, then, was there a place for him
That on this other side of death
Saw nothing good, as he had seen
No good come out of Nazareth?

Yet here there was a reticence,
And I believe his only one,
That hushed him as if he beheld
A Presence that would not be gone.
In such a silence he confessed
How much there was to be denied;
And he would look at me and live,
As others might have looked and died.

As if at last he knew again
That he had always known, his eyes
Were like to those of one who gazed
On those of One who never dies.
For such a moment he revealed
What life has in it to be lost;
And I could ask if what I saw,
Before me there, was man or ghost.

He may have died so many times
That all there was of him to see
Was pride, that kept itself alive
As too rebellious to be free;
He may have told, when more than once
Humility seemed imminent,
How many a lonely time in vain
The Second Coming came and went.

Whether he still defies or not
The failure of an angry task
That relegates him out of time

To chaos, I can only ask.
But as I knew him, so he was;
And somewhere among men to-day
Those old, unyielding eyes may flash,
And flinch—and look the other way.

NEIGHBORS

As often as we thought of her,
　　We thought of a gray life
That made a quaint economist
　　Of a wolf-haunted wife;
We made the best of all she bore
　　That was not ours to bear,
And honored her for wearing things
　　That were not things to wear.

There was a distance in her look
　　That made us look again;
And if she smiled, we might believe
　　That we had looked in vain.
Rarely she came inside our doors,
　　And had not long to stay;
And when she left, it seemed somehow
　　That she was far away.

At last, when we had all forgot
　　That all is here to change,
A shadow on the commonplace
　　Was for a moment strange.
Yet there was nothing for surprise,
　　Nor much that need be told:
Love, with his gift of pain, had given
　　More than one heart could hold.

THE MILL

The miller's wife had waited long,
   The tea was cold, the fire was dead;
And there might yet be nothing wrong
   In how he went and what he said:
"There are no millers any more,"
   Was all that she had heard him say;
And he had lingered at the door
   So long that it seemed yesterday.

Sick with a fear that had no form
   She knew that she was there at last;
And in the mill there was a warm
   And mealy fragrance of the past.
What else there was would only seem
   To say again what he had meant;
And what was hanging from a beam
   Would not have heeded where she went.

And if she thought it followed her,
   She may have reasoned in the dark
That one way of the few there were
   Would hide her and would leave no mark:
Black water, smooth above the weir
   Like starry velvet in the night,
Though ruffled once, would soon appear
   The same as ever to the sight.

THE DARK HILLS

Dark hills at evening in the west,
Where sunset hovers like a sound
Of golden horns that sang to rest
Old bones of warriors under ground,
Far now from all the bannered ways
Where flash the legions of the sun,
You fade—as if the last of days
Were fading, and all wars were done.

THE THREE TAVERNS

When the brethren heard of us, they came to meet us as far as
Appii Forum, and The Three Taverns.

(Acts xxviii, 15)

Herodion, Apelles, Amplias,
And Andronicus? Is it you I see—
At last? And is it you now that are gazing
As if in doubt of me? Was I not saying
That I should come to Rome? I did say that;
And I said furthermore that I should go
On westward, where the gateway of the world
Lets in the central sea. I did say that,
But I say only, now, that I am Paul—
A prisoner of the Law, and of the Lord
A voice made free. If there be time enough
To live, I may have more to tell you then
Of western matters. I go now to Rome,
Where Cæsar waits for me, and I shall wait,
And Cæsar knows how long. In Cæsarea
There was a legend of Agrippa saying
In a light way to Festus, having heard
My deposition, that I might be free,
Had I stayed free of Cæsar; but the word
Of God would have it as you see it is—
And here I am. The cup that I shall drink
Is mine to drink—the moment or the place
Not mine to say. If it be now in Rome,
Be it now in Rome; and if your faith exceed
The shadow cast of hope, say not of me
Too surely or too soon that years and shipwreck,
And all the many deserts I have crossed
That are not named or regioned, have undone
Beyond the brevities of our mortal healing

The part of me that is the least of me.
You see an older man than he who fell
Prone to the earth when he was nigh Damascus,
Where the great light came down; yet I am he
That fell, and he that saw, and he that heard.
And I am here, at last; and if at last
I give myself to make another crumb
For this pernicious feast of time and men—
Well, I have seen too much of time and men
To fear the ravening or the wrath of either.

Yes, it is Paul you see—the Saul of Tarsus
That was a fiery Jew, and had men slain
For saying Something was beyond the Law,
And in ourselves. I fed my suffering soul
Upon the Law till I went famishing,
Not knowing that I starved. How should I know,
More then than any, that the food I had—
What else it may have been—was not for me?
My fathers and their fathers and their fathers
Had found it good, and said there was no other,
And I was of the line. When Stephen fell,
Among the stones that crushed his life away,
There was no place alive that I could see
For such a man. Why should a man be given
To live beyond the Law? So I said then,
As men say now to me. How then do I
Persist in living? Is that what you ask?
If so, let my appearance be for you
No living answer; for Time writes of death
On men before they die, and what you see
Is not the man. The man that you see not—
The man within the man—is most alive;

Though hatred would have ended, long ago,
The bane of his activities. I have lived,
Because the faith within me that is life
Endures to live, and shall, till soon or late,
Death, like a friend unseen, shall say to me
My toil is over and my work begun.

How often, and how many a time again,
Have I said I should be with you in Rome!
He who is always coming never comes,
Or comes too late, you may have told yourselves;
And I may tell you now that after me,
Whether I stay for little or for long,
The wolves are coming. Have an eye for them,
And a more careful ear for their confusion
Than you need have much longer for the sound
Of what I tell you—should I live to say
More than I say to Cæsar. What I know
Is down for you to read in what is written;
And if I cloud a little with my own
Mortality the gleam that is immortal,
I do it only because I am I—
Being on earth and of it, in so far
As time flays yet the remnant. This you know;
And if I sting men, as I do sometimes,
With a sharp word that hurts, it is because
Man's habit is to feel before he sees;
And I am of a race that feels. Moreover,
The world is here for what is not yet here
For more than are a few; and even in Rome,
Where men are so enamored of the Cross
That fame has echoed, and increasingly,
The music of your love and of your faith

To foreign ears that are as far away
As Antioch and Haran, yet I wonder
How much of love you know, and if your faith
Be the shut fruit of words. If so, remember
Words are but shells unfilled. Jews have at least
A Law to make them sorry they were born
If they go long without it; and these Gentiles,
For the first time in shrieking history,
Have love and law together, if so they will,
For their defense and their immunity
In these last days. Rome, if I know the name,
Will have anon a crown of thorns and fire
Made ready for the wreathing of new masters,
Of whom we are appointed, you and I,—
And you are still to be when I am gone,
Should I go presently. Let the word fall,
Meanwhile, upon the dragon-ridden field
Of circumstance, either to live or die;
Concerning which there is a parable,
Made easy for the comfort and attention
Of those who preach, fearing they preach in vain.
You are to plant, and then to plant again
Where you have gathered, gathering as you go;
For you are in the fields that are eternal,
And you have not the burden of the Lord
Upon your mortal shoulders. What you have
Is a light yoke, made lighter by the wearing,
Till it shall have the wonder and the weight
Of a clear jewel, shining with a light
Wherein the sun and all the fiery stars
May soon be fading. When Gamaliel said
That if they be of men these things are nothing,
But if they be of God, they are for none

To overthrow, he spoke as a good Jew,
And one who stayed a Jew; and he said all.
And you know, by the temper of your faith,
How far the fire is in you that I felt
Before I knew Damascus. A word here,
Or there, or not there, or not anywhere,
Is not the Word that lives and is the life;
And you, therefore, need weary not yourselves
With jealous aches of others. If the world
Were not a world of aches and innovations,
Attainment would have no more joy of it.
There will be creeds and schisms, creeds in creeds,
And schisms in schisms; myriads will be done
To death because a farthing has two sides,
And is at last a farthing. Telling you this,
I, who bid men to live, appeal to Cæsar.
Once I had said the ways of God were dark,
Meaning by that the dark ways of the Law.
Such is the Glory of our tribulations;
For the Law kills the flesh that kills the Law,
And we are then alive. We have eyes then;
And we have then the Cross between two worlds—
To guide us, or to blind us for a time,
Till we have eyes indeed. The fire that smites
A few on highways, changing all at once,
Is not for all. The power that holds the world
Away from God that holds himself away—
Farther away than all your works and words
Are like to fly without the wings of faith—
Was not, nor ever shall be, a small hazard
Enlivening the ways of easy leisure
Or the cold road of knowledge. When our eyes
Have wisdom, we see more than we remember;

And the old world of our captivities
May then become a smitten glimpse of ruin,
Like one where vanished hewers have had their day
Of wrath on Lebanon. Before we see,
Meanwhile, we suffer; and I come to you,
At last, through many storms and through much night.

Yet whatsoever I have undergone,
My keepers in this instance are not hard.
But for the chance of an ingratitude,
I might indeed be curious of their mercy,
And fearful of their leisure while I wait,
A few leagues out of Rome. Men go to Rome,
Not always to return—but not that now.
Meanwhile, I seem to think you look at me
With eyes that are at last more credulous
Of my identity. You remark in me
No sort of leaping giant, though some words
Of mine to you from Corinth may have leapt
A little through your eyes into your soul.
I trust they were alive, and are alive
Today; for there be none that shall indite
So much of nothing as the man of words
Who writes in the Lord's name for his name's sake
And has not in his blood the fire of time
To warm eternity. Let such a man—
If once the light is in him and endures—
Content himself to be the general man,
Set free to sift the decencies and thereby
To learn, except he be one set aside
For sorrow, more of pleasure than of pain;
Though if his light be not the light indeed,
But a brief shine that never really was,
And fails, leaving him worse than where he was,

Then shall he be of all men destitute.
And here were not an issue for much ink,
Or much offending faction among scribes.

The Kingdom is within us, we are told;
And when I say to you that we possess it
In such a measure as faith makes it ours,
I say it with a sinner's privilege
Of having seen and heard, and seen again,
After a darkness; and if I affirm
To the last hour that faith affords alone
The Kingdom entrance and an entertainment,
I do not see myself as one who says
To man that he shall sit with folded hands
Against the Coming. If I be anything,
I move a driven agent among my kind,
Establishing by the faith of Abraham,
And by the grace of their necessities,
The clamoring word that is the word of life
Nearer than heretofore to the solution
Of their tomb-serving doubts. If I have loosed
A shaft of language that has flown sometimes
A little higher than the hearts and heads
Of nature's minions, it will yet be heard,
Like a new song that waits for distant ears.
I cannot be the man that I am not;
And while I own that earth is my affliction,
I am a man of earth, who says not all
To all alike. That were impossible,
Even as it were so that He should plant
A larger garden first. But you today
Are for the larger sowing; and your seed,
A little mixed, will have, as He foresaw,
The foreign harvest of a wider growth,

And one without an end. Many there are,
And are to be, that shall partake of it,
Though none may share it with an understanding
That is not his alone. We are all alone;
And yet we are all parcelled of one order—
Jew, Gentile, or barbarian in the dark
Of wildernesses that are not so much
As names yet in a book. And there are many,
Finding at last that words are not the Word,
And finding only that, will flourish aloft,
Like heads of captured Pharisees on pikes,
Our contradictions and discrepancies;
And there are many more will hang themselves
Upon the letter, seeing not in the Word
The friend of all who fail, and in their faith
A sword of excellence to cut them down.

As long as there are glasses that are dark—
And there are many—we see darkly through them;
All which have I conceded and set down
In words that have no shadow. What is dark
Is dark, and we may not say otherwise;
Yet what may be as dark as a lost fire
For one of us, may still be for another
A coming gleam across the gulf of ages,
And a way home from shipwreck to the shore;
And so, through pangs and ills and desperations,
There may be light for all. There shall be light.
As much as that, you know. You cannot say
This woman or that man will be the next
On whom it falls; you are not here for that.
Your ministration is to be for others
The firing of a rush that may for them
Be soon the fire itself. The few at first

Are fighting for the multitude at last;
Therefore remember what Gamaliel said
Before you, when the sick were lying down
In streets all night for Peter's passing shadow.
Fight, and say what you feel; say more than words.
Give men to know that even their days of earth
To come are more than ages that are gone.
Say what you feel, while you have time to say it.
Eternity will answer for itself,
Without your intercession; yet the way
For many is a long one, and as dark,
Meanwhile, as dreams of hell. See not your toil
Too much, and if I be away from you,
Think of me as a brother to yourselves,
Of many blemishes. Beware of stoics,
And give your left hand to grammarians;
And when you seem, as many a time you may,
To have no other friend than hope, remember
That you are not the first, or yet the last.

The best of life, until we see beyond
The shadows of ourselves (and they are less
Than even the blindest of indignant eyes
Would have them) is in what we do not know.
Make, then, for all your fears a place to sleep
With all your faded sins; nor think yourselves
Egregious and alone for your defects
Of youth and yesterday. I was young once;
And there's a question if you played the fool
With a more fervid and inherent zeal
Than I have in my story to remember,
Or gave your necks to folly's conquering foot,
Or flung yourselves with an unstudied aim,
More frequently than I. Never mind that.

Man's little house of days will hold enough,
Sometimes, to make him wish it were not his,
But it will not hold all. Things that are dead
Are best without it, and they own their death
By virtue of their dying. Let them go,—
But think you not the world is ashes yet,
And you have all the fire. The world is here
Today, and it may not be gone tomorrow;
For there are millions, and there may be more,
To make in turn a various estimation
Of its old ills and ashes, and the traps
Of its apparent wrath. Many with ears
That hear not yet, shall have ears given to them,
And then they shall hear strangely. Many with eyes
That are incredulous of the Mystery
Shall yet be driven to feel, and then to read
Where language has an end and is a veil,
Not woven of our words. Many that hate
Their kind are soon to know that without love
Their faith is but the perjured name of nothing.
I that have done some hating in my time
See now no time for hate; I that have left,
Fading behind me like familiar lights
That are to shine no more for my returning,
Home, friends, and honors,—I that have lost all else
For wisdom, and the wealth of it, say now
To you that out of wisdom has come love,
That measures and is of itself the measure
Of works and hope and faith. Your longest hours
Are not so long that you may torture them
And harass not yourselves; and the last days
Are on the way that you prepare for them,
And was prepared for you, here in a world
Where you have sinned and suffered, striven and seen.

If you be not so hot for counting them
Before they come that you consume yourselves,
Peace may attend you all in these last days—
And me, as well as you. Yes, even in Rome.

Well, I have talked and rested, though I fear
My rest has not been yours; in which event,
Forgive one who is only seven leagues
From Cæsar. When I told you I should come,
I did not see myself the criminal
You contemplate, for seeing beyond the Law
That which the Law saw not. But this, indeed,
Was good of you, and I shall not forget;
No, I shall not forget you came so far
To meet a man so dangerous. Well, farewell.
They come to tell me I am going now—
With them. I hope that we shall meet again,
But none may say what he shall find in Rome.

THE FLYING DUTCHMAN

Unyielding in the pride of his defiance,
    Afloat with none to serve or to command,
Lord of himself at last, and all by Science,
    He seeks the Vanished Land.

Alone, by the one light of his one thought,
    He steers to find the shore from which we came,
Fearless of in what coil he may be caught
    On seas that have no name.

Into the night he sails; and after night
    There is a dawning, though there be no sun;
Wherefore, with nothing but himself in sight,
    Unsighted, he sails on.

At last there is a lifting of the cloud
    Between the flood before him and the sky;
And then—though he may curse the Power aloud
    That has no power to die—

He steers himself away from what is haunted
    By the old ghost of what has been before,—
Abandoning, as always, and undaunted,
    One fog-walled island more.

TACT

Observant of the way she told
   So much of what was true,
No vanity could long withhold
   Regard that was her due:
She spared him the familiar guile,
   So easily achieved,
That only made a man to smile
   And left him undeceived.

Aware that all imagining
   Of more than what she meant
Would urge an end of everything,
   He stayed; and when he went,
They parted with a merry word
   That was to him as light
As any that was ever heard
   Upon a starry night.

She smiled a little, knowing well
   That he would not remark
The ruins of a day that fell
   Around her in the dark:
He saw no ruins anywhere,
   Nor fancied there were scars
On anyone who lingered there,
   Alone below the stars.

JOHN BROWN

Though for your sake I would not have you now
So near to me tonight as now you are,
God knows how much a stranger to my heart
Was any cold word that I may have written;
And you, poor woman that I made my wife,
You have had more of loneliness, I fear,
Than I—though I have been the most alone,
Even when the most attended. So it was
God set the mark of his inscrutable
Necessity on one that was to grope,
And serve, and suffer, and withal be glad
For what was his, and is, and is to be,
When his old bones, that are a burden now,
Are saying what the man who carried them
Had not the power to say. Bones in a grave,
Cover them as they will with choking earth,
May shout the truth to men who put them there,
More than all orators. And so, my dear,
Since you have cheated wisdom for the sake
Of sorrow, let your sorrow be for you,
This last of nights before the last of days,
The lying ghost of what there is of me
That is the most alive. There is no death
For me in what they do. Their death it is
They should heed most when the sun comes again
To make them solemn. There are some I know
Whose eyes will hardly see their occupation,
For tears in them—and all for one old man;
For some of them will pity this old man,
Who took upon himself the work of God
Because he pitied millions. That will be
For them, I fancy, their compassionate

Best way of saying what is best in them
To say; for they can say no more than that,
And they can do no more than what the dawn
Of one more day shall give them light enough
To do. But there are many days to be,
And there are many men to give their blood,
As I gave mine for them. May they come soon!

May they come soon, I say. And when they come,
May all that I have said unheard be heard,
Proving at last, or maybe not—no matter—
What sort of madness was the part of me
That made me strike, whether I found the mark
Or missed it. Meanwhile, I've a strange content,
A patience, and a vast indifference
To what men say of me and what men fear
To say. There was a work to be begun,
And when the Voice, that I have heard so long,
Announced as in a thousand silences
An end of preparation, I began
The coming work of death which is to be,
That life may be. There is no other way
Than the old way of war for a new land
That will not know itself and is tonight
A stranger to itself, and to the world
A more prodigious upstart among states
Than I was among men, and so shall be
Till they are told and told, and told again;
For men are children, waiting to be told,
And most of them are children all their lives.
The good God in his wisdom had them so,
That now and then a madman or a seer
May shake them out of their complacency
And shame them into deeds. The major file

See only what their fathers may have seen,
Or may have said they saw when they saw nothing.
I do not say it matters what they saw.
Now and again to some lone soul or other
God speaks, and there is hanging to be done,—
As once there was a burning of our bodies
Alive, albeit our souls were sorry fuel.
But now the fires are few, and we are poised
Accordingly, for the state's benefit,
A few still minutes between heaven and earth.
The purpose is, when they have seen enough
Of what it is that they are not to see,
To pluck me as an unripe fruit of treason,
And then to fling me back to the same earth
Of which they are, as I suppose, the flower—
Not given to know the riper fruit that waits
For a more comprehensive harvesting.

Yes, may they come, and soon. Again I say,
May they come soon!—before too many of them
Shall be the bloody cost of our defection.
When hell waits on the dawn of a new state,
Better it were that hell should not wait long,—
Or so it is I see it who should see
As far or farther into time tonight
Than they who talk and tremble for me now,
Or wish me to those everlasting fires
That are for me no fear. Too many fires
Have sought me out and seared me to the bone—
Thereby, for all I know, to temper me
For what was mine to do. If I did ill
What I did well, let men say I was mad;
Or let my name for ever be a question

That will not sleep in history. What men say
I was will cool no cannon, dull no sword,
Invalidate no truth. Meanwhile, I was;
And the long train is lighted that shall burn,
Though floods of wrath may drench it, and hot feet
May stamp it for a slight time into smoke
That shall blaze up again with growing speed,
Until at last a fiery crash will come
To cleanse and shake a wounded hemisphere,
And heal it of a long malignity
That angry time discredits and disowns.

Tonight there are men saying many things;
And some who see life in the last of me
Will answer first the coming call to death;
For death is what is coming, and then life.
I do not say again for the dull sake
Of speech what you have heard me say before,
But rather for the sake of all I am,
And all God made of me. A man to die
As I do must have done some other work
Than man's alone. I was not after glory,
But there was glory with me, like a friend,
Throughout those crippling years when friends were few,
And fearful to be known by their own names
When mine was vilified for their approval.
Yet friends they are, and they did what was given
Their will to do; they could have done no more.
I was the one man mad enough, it seems,
To do my work; and now my work is over.
And you, my dear, are not to mourn for me,
Or for your sons, more than a soul should mourn
In Paradise, done with evil and with earth.

There is not much of earth in what remains
For you; and what there may be left of it
For your endurance you shall have at last
In peace, without the twinge of any fear
For my condition; for I shall be done
With plans and actions that have heretofore
Made your days long and your nights ominous
With darkness and the many distances
That were between us. When the silence comes,
I shall in faith be nearer to you then
Than I am now in fact. What you see now
Is only the outside of an old man,
Older than years have made him. Let him die,
And let him be a thing for little grief.
There was a time for service and he served;
And there is no more time for anything
But a short gratefulness to those who gave
Their scared allegiance to an enterprise
That has the name of treason—which will serve
As well as any other for the present.
There are some deeds of men that have no names,
And mine may like as not be one of them.
I am not looking far for names tonight.
The King of Glory was without a name
Until men gave Him one; yet there He was,
Before we found Him and affronted Him
With numerous ingenuities of evil,
Of which one, with His aid, is to be swept
And washed out of the world with fire and blood.

Once I believed it might have come to pass
With a small cost of blood; but I was dreaming—
Dreaming that I believed. The Voice I heard
When I left you behind me in the north,—
To wait there and to wonder and grow old
Of loneliness,—told only what was best,
And with a saving vagueness, I should know
Till I knew more. And had I known even then—
After grim years of search and suffering,
So many of them to end as they began—
After my sickening doubts and estimations
Of plans abandoned and of new plans vain—
After a weary delving everywhere
For men with every virtue but the Vision—
Could I have known, I say, before I left you
That summer morning, all there was to know—
Even unto the last consuming word
That would have blasted every mortal answer
As lightning would annihilate a leaf,
I might have trembled on that summer morning;
I might have wavered; and I might have failed.

And there are many among men today
To say of me that I had best have wavered.
So has it been, so shall it always be,
For those of us who give ourselves to die
Before we are so parcelled and approved
As to be slaughtered by authority.
We do not make so much of what they say
As they of what our folly says of us;
They give us hardly time enough for that,

And thereby we gain much by losing little.
Few are alive today with less to lose
Than I who tell you this, or more to gain;
And whether I speak as one to be destroyed
For no good end outside his own destruction,
Time shall have more to say than men shall hear
Between now and the coming of that harvest
Which is to come. Before it comes, I go—
By the short road that mystery makes long
For man's endurance of accomplishment.
I shall have more to say when I am dead.

ARCHIBALD'S EXAMPLE

Old Archibald, in his eternal chair,
Where trespassers, whatever their degree,
Were soon frowned out again, was looking off
Across the clover when he said to me:

"My green hill yonder, where the sun goes down
Without a scratch, was once inhabited
By trees that injured him—an evil trash
That made a cage, and held him while he bled.

"Gone fifty years, I see them as they were
Before they fell. They were a crooked lot
To spoil my sunset, and I saw no time
In fifty years for crooked things to rot.

"Trees, yes; but not a service or a joy
To God or man, for they were thieves of light.
So down they came. Nature and I looked on,
And we were glad when they were out of sight.

"Trees are like men, sometimes; and that being so,
So much for that." He twinkled in his chair,
And looked across the clover to the place
That he remembered when the trees were there.

A SONG AT SHANNON'S

Two men came out of Shannon's, having known
The faces of each other for as long
As they had listened there to an old song,
Sung thinly in a wastrel monotone
By some unhappy night-bird, who had flown
Too many times and with a wing too strong
To save himself, and so done heavy wrong
To more frail elements than his alone.

Slowly away they went, leaving behind
More light than was before them. Neither met
The other's eyes again or said a word.
Each to his loneliness or to his kind,
Went his own way, and with his own regret,
Not knowing what the other may have heard.

SOUVENIR

A vanished house that for an hour I knew
By some forgotten chance when I was young
Had once a glimmering window overhung
With honeysuckle wet with evening dew.
Along the path tall dusky dahlias grew,
And shadowy hydrangeas reached and swung
Ferociously; and over me, among
The moths and mysteries, a blurred bat flew.

Somewhere within there were dim presences
Of days that hovered and of years gone by.
I waited, and between their silences
There was an evanescent faded noise;
And though a child, I knew it was the voice
Of one whose occupation was to die.

FIRELIGHT

Ten years together without yet a cloud,
They seek each other's eyes at intervals
Of gratefulness to firelight and four walls
For love's obliteration of the crowd.
Serenely and perennially endowed
And bowered as few may be, their joy recalls
No snake, no sword; and over them there falls
The blessing of what neither says aloud.

Wiser for silence, they were not so glad
Were she to read the graven tale of lines
On the wan face of one somewhere alone;
Nor were they more content could he have had
Her thoughts a moment since of one who shines
Apart, and would be hers if he had known.

LATE SUMMER

(Alcaics)

Confused, he found her lavishing feminine
Gold upon clay, and found her inscrutable;
    And yet she smiled. Why, then, should horrors
Be as they were, without end, her playthings?

And why were dead years hungrily telling her
Lies of the dead, who told them again to her?
    If now she knew, there might be kindness
Clamoring yet where a faith lay stifled.

A little faith in him, and the ruinous
Past would be for time to annihilate,
    And wash out, like a tide that washes
Out of the sand what a child has drawn there.

God, what a shining handful of happiness,
Made out of days and out of eternities,
    Were now the pulsing end of patience—
Could he but have what a ghost had stolen!

What was a man before him, or ten of them,
While he was here alive who could answer them,
    And in their teeth fling confirmations
Harder than agates against an egg-shell?

But now the man was dead, and would come again
Never, though she might honor ineffably
    The flimsy wraith of him she conjured
Out of a dream with his wand of absence.

And if the truth were now but a mummery,
Meriting pride's implacable irony,
    So much the worse for pride. Moreover,
Save her or fail, there was conscience always.

Meanwhile, a few misgivings of innocence,
Imploring to be sheltered and credited,
    Were not amiss when she revealed them.
Whether she struggled or not, he saw them.

Also, he saw that while she was hearing him
Her eyes had more and more of the past in them;
    And while he told what cautious honor
Told him was all he had best be sure of,

He wondered once or twice, inadvertently,
Where shifting winds were driving his argosies,
    Long anchored and as long unladen,
Over the foam for the golden chances.

"If men were not for killing so carelessly,
And women were for wiser endurances,"
    He said, "we might have yet a world here
Fitter for Truth to be seen abroad in;

"If Truth were not so strange in her nakedness,
And we were less forbidden to look at it,
    We might not have to look." He stared then
Down at the sand where the tide threw forward

Its cold, unconquered lines, that unceasingly
Foamed against hope, and fell. He was calm enough,
    Although he knew he might be silenced
Out of all calm; and the night was coming.

"I climb for you the peak of his infamy
That you may choose your fall if you cling to it.
    No more for me unless you say more.
All you have left of a dream defends you:

"The truth may be as evil an augury
As it was needful now for the two of us.
    We cannot have the dead between us.
Tell me to go, and I go."—She pondered:

"What you believe is right for the two of us
Makes it as right that you are not one of us.
    If this be needful truth you tell me,
Spare me, and let me have lies hereafter."

She gazed away where shadows were covering
The whole cold ocean's healing indifference.
    No ship was coming. When the darkness
Fell, she was there, and alone, still gazing.

A VON'S HARVEST, ETC.

MR. FLOOD'S PARTY

Old Eben Flood, climbing alone one night
Over the hill between the town below
And the forsaken upland hermitage
That held as much as he should ever know
On earth again of home, paused warily.
The road was his with not a native near;
And Eben, having leisure, said aloud,
For no man else in Tilbury Town to hear:

"Well, Mr. Flood, we have the harvest moon
Again, and we may not have many more;
The bird is on the wing, the poet says,
And you and I have said it here before.
Drink to the bird." He raised up to the light
The jug that he had gone so far to fill,
And answered huskily: "Well, Mr. Flood,
Since you propose it, I believe I will."

Alone, as if enduring to the end
A valiant armor of scarred hopes outworn,
He stood there in the middle of the road
Like Roland's ghost winding a silent horn.
Below him, in the town among the trees,
Where friends of other days had honored him,
A phantom salutation of the dead
Rang thinly till old Eben's eyes were dim.

Then, as a mother lays her sleeping child
Down tenderly, fearing it may awake,
He set the jug down slowly at his feet
With trembling care, knowing that most things break;
And only when assured that on firm earth

It stood, as the uncertain lives of men
Assuredly did not, he paced away,
And with his hand extended paused again:

"Well, Mr. Flood, we have not met like this
In a long time; and many a change has come
To both of us, I fear, since last it was
We had a drop together. Welcome home!"
Convivially returning with himself,
Again he raised the jug up to the light;
And with an acquiescent quaver said:
"Well, Mr. Flood, if you insist, I might.

"Only a very little, Mr. Flood—
For auld lang syne. No more, sir; that will do."
So, for the time, apparently it did,
And Eben evidently thought so too;
For soon amid the silver loneliness
Of night he lifted up his voice and sang,
Secure, with only two moons listening,
Until the whole harmonious landscape rang—

"For auld lang syne." The weary throat gave out,
The last word wavered, and the song was done.
He raised again the jug regretfully
And shook his head, and was again alone.
There was not much that was ahead of him,
And there was nothing in the town below—
Where strangers would have shut the many doors
That many friends had opened long ago.

BEN TROVATO

The deacon thought. "I know them," he began,
"And they are all you ever heard of them—
Allurable to no sure theorem,
The scorn or the humility of man.
You say 'Can I believe it?'—and I can;
And I'm unwilling even to condemn
The benefaction of a stratagem
Like hers—and I'm a Presbyterian.

"Though blind, with but a wandering hour to live,
He felt the other woman in the fur
That now the wife had on. Could she forgive
All that? Apparently. Her rings were gone,
Of course; and when he found that she had none,
He smiled—as he had never smiled at her."

THE TREE IN PAMELA'S GARDEN

Pamela was too gentle to deceive
Her roses. "Let the men stay where they are,"
She said, "and if Apollo's avatar
Be one of them, I shall not have to grieve."
And so she made all Tilbury Town believe
She sighed a little more for the North Star
Than over men, and only in so far
As she was in a garden was like Eve.

Her neighbors—doing all that neighbors can
To make romance of reticence meanwhile—
Seeing that she had never loved a man,
Wished Pamela had a cat, or a small bird,
And only would have wondered at her smile
Could they have seen that she had overheard.

VAIN GRATUITIES

Never was there a man much uglier
In eyes of other women, or more grim:
"The Lord has filled her chalice to the brim,
So let us pray she's a philosopher,"
They said; and there was more they said of her—
Deeming it, after twenty years with him,
No wonder that she kept her figure slim
And always made you think of lavender.

But she, demure as ever, and as fair,
Almost, as they remembered her before
She found him, would have laughed had she been there;
And all they said would have been heard no more
Than foam that washes on an island shore
Where there are none to listen or to care.

LOST ANCHORS

Like a dry fish flung inland far from shore,
There lived a sailor, warped and ocean-browned,
Who told of an old vessel, harbor-drowned
And out of mind a century before,
Where divers, on descending to explore
A legend that had lived its way around
The world of ships, in the dark hulk had found
Anchors, which had been seized and seen no more.

Improving a dry leisure to invest
Their misadventure with a manifest
Analogy that he may read who runs,
The sailor made it old as ocean grass—
Telling of much that once had come to pass
With him, whose mother should have had no sons.

RECALLED

Long after there were none of them alive
About the place—where there is now no place
But a walled hole where fruitless vines embrace
Their parent skeletons that yet survive
In evil thorns—none of us could arrive
At a more cogent answer to their ways
Than one old Isaac in his latter days
Had humor or compassion to contrive.

I mentioned them, and Isaac shook his head:
"The Power that you call yours and I call mine
Extinguished in the last of them a line
That Satan would have disinherited.
When we are done with all but the Divine,
We die." And there was no more to be said.

AFTERTHOUGHTS

We parted where the old gas-lamp still burned
Under the wayside maple and walked on,
Into the dark, as we had always done;
And I, no doubt, if he had not returned,
Might yet be unaware that he had earned
More than earth gives to many who have won
More than it has to give when they are gone—
As duly and indelibly I learned.

The sum of all that he came back to say
Was little then, and would be less today:
With him there were no Delphic heights to climb,
Yet his were somehow nearer the sublime.
He spoke, and went again by the old way—
Not knowing it would be for the last time.

CAPUT MORTUUM

Not even if with a wizard force I might
Have summoned whomsoever I would name,
Should anyone else have come than he who came,
Uncalled, to share with me my fire that night;
For though I should have said that all was right,
Or right enough, nothing had been the same
As when I found him there before the flame,
Always a welcome and a useful sight.

Unfailing and exuberant all the time,
Having no gold he paid with golden rhyme,
Of older coinage than his old defeat,
A debt that like himself was obsolete
In Art's long hazard, where no man may choose
Whether he play to win or toil to lose.

MONADNOCK THROUGH THE TREES

Before there was in Egypt any sound
Of those who reared a more prodigious means
For the self-heavy sleep of kings and queens
Than hitherto had mocked the most renowned,—
Unvisioned here and waiting to be found,
Alone, amid remote and older scenes,
You loomed above ancestral evergreens
Before there were the first of us around.

And when the last of us, if we know how,
See farther from ourselves than we do now,
Assured with other sight than heretofore
That we have done our mortal best and worst,—
Your calm will be the same as when the first
Assyrians went howling south to war.

THE LONG RACE

Up the old hill to the old house again
Where fifty years ago the friend was young
Who should be waiting somewhere there among
Old things that least remembered most remain,
He toiled on with a pleasure that was pain
To think how soon asunder would be flung
The curtain half a century had hung
Between the two ambitions they had slain.

They dredged an hour for words, and then were done.
"Good-bye! . . . You have the same old weather-vane—
Your little horse that's always on the run."
And all the way down back to the next train,
Down the old hill to the old road again,
It seemed as if the little horse had won.

MANY ARE CALLED

The Lord Apollo, who has never died,
Still holds alone his immemorial reign,
Supreme in an impregnable domain
That with his magic he has fortified;
And though melodious multitudes have tried
In ecstasy, in anguish, and in vain,
With invocation sacred and profane
To lure him, even the loudest are outside.

Only at unconjectured intervals,
By will of him on whom no man may gaze,
By word of him whose law no man has read,
A questing light may rift the sullen walls,
To cling where mostly its infrequent rays
Fall golden on the patience of the dead.

REMBRANDT TO REMBRANDT

(Amsterdam, 1645)

And there you are again, now as you are.
Observe yourself as you discern yourself
In your discredited ascendency;
Without your velvet or your feathers now,
Commend your new condition to your fate,
And your conviction to the sieves of time.
Meanwhile appraise yourself, Rembrandt van Ryn,
Now as you are—formerly more or less
Distinguished in the civil scenery,
And once a painter. There you are again,
Where you may see that you have on your shoulders
No lovelier burden for an ornament
Than one man's head that's yours. Praise be to God
That you have that; for you are like enough
To need it now, my friend, and from now on;
For there are shadows and obscurities
Immediate or impending on your view,
That may be worse than you have ever painted
For the bewildered and unhappy scorn
Of injured Hollanders in Amsterdam
Who cannot find their fifty florins' worth
Of Holland face where you have hidden it
In your new golden shadow that excites them,
Or see that when the Lord made color and light
He made not one thing only, or believe
That shadows are not nothing. Saskia said,
Before she died, how they would swear at you,
And in commiseration at themselves.
She laughed a little, too, to think of them—
And then at me. . . . That was before she died.

And I could wonder, as I look at you,
There as I have you now, there as you are,
Or nearly so as any skill of mine
Has ever caught you in a bilious mirror,—
Yes, I could wonder long, and with a reason,
If all but everything achievable
In me were not achieved and lost already,
Like a fool's gold. But you there in the glass,
And you there on the canvas, have a sort
Of solemn doubt about it; and that's well
For Rembrandt and for Titus. All that's left
Of all that was is here; and all that's here
Is one man who remembers, and one child
Beginning to forget. One, two, and three,
The others died, and then—then Saskia died;
And then, so men believe, the painter died.
So men believe. So it all comes at once.
And here's a fellow painting in the dark,—
A loon who cannot see that he is dead
Before God lets him die. He paints away
At the impossible, so Holland has it,
For venom or for spite, or for defection,
Or else for God knows what. Well, if God knows,
And Rembrandt knows, it matters not so much
What Holland knows or cares. If Holland wants
Its heads all in a row, and all alike,
There's Franz to do them and to do them well—
Rat-catchers, archers, or apothecaries,
And one as like a rabbit as another.
Value received, and every Dutchman happy.
All's one to Franz, and to the rest of them,—
Their ways being theirs, are theirs.—But you, my friend,

If I have made you something as you are,
Will need those jaws and eyes and all the fight
And fire that's in them, and a little more,
To take you on and the world after you;
For now you fare alone, without the fashion
To sing you back and fling a flower or two
At your accusing feet. Poor Saskia saw
This coming that has come, and with a guile
Of kindliness that covered half her doubts
Would give me gold, and laugh . . . before she died.

And if I see the road that you are going,
You that are not so jaunty as aforetime,
God knows if she were not appointed well
To die. She might have wearied of it all
Before the worst was over, or begun.
A woman waiting on a man's avouch
Of the invisible, may not wait always
Without a word betweenwhiles, or a dash
Of poison on his faith. Yes, even she.
She might have come to see at last with others,
And then to say with others, who say more,
That you are groping on a phantom trail
Determining a dusky way to nowhere;
That errors unconfessed and obstinate
Have teemed and cankered in you for so long
That even your eyes are sick, and you see light
Only because you dare not see the dark
That is around you and ahead of you.
She might have come, by ruinous estimation
Of old applause and outworn vanities,
To clothe you over in a shroud of dreams,
And so be nearer to the counterfeit
Of her invention than aware of yours.

She might, as well as any, by this time,
Unwillingly and eagerly have bitten
Another devil's-apple of unrest,
And so, by some attendant artifice
Or other, might anon have had you sharing
A taste that would have tainted everything,
And so had been for two, instead of one,
The taste of death in life—which is the food
Of art that has betrayed itself alive
And is a food of hell. She might have heard
Unhappily the temporary noise
Of louder names than yours, and on frail urns
That hardly will ensure a dwelling-place
For even the dust that may be left of them,
She might, and angrily, as like as not,
Look soon to find your name, not finding it.
She might, like many another born for joy
And for sufficient fulness of the hour,
Go famishing by now, and in the eyes
Of pitying friends and dwindling satellites
Be told of no uncertain dereliction
Touching the cold offence of my decline.
And even if this were so, and she were here
Again to make a fact of all my fancy,
How should I ask of her to see with me
Through night where many a time I seem in vain
To seek for new assurance of a gleam
That comes at last, and then, so it appears,
Only for you and me—and a few more,
Perchance, albeit their faces are not many
Among the ruins that are now around us.
That was a fall, my friend, we had together—
Or rather it was my house, mine alone,
That fell, leaving you safe. Be glad for that.

There's life in you that shall outlive my clay
That's for a time alive and will in time
Be nothing—but not yet. You that are there
Where I have painted you are safe enough,
Though I see dragons. Verily, that was a fall—
A dislocating fall, a blinding fall,
A fall indeed. But there are no bones broken;
And even the teeth and eyes that I make out
Among the shadows, intermittently,
Show not so firm in their accoutrement
Of terror-laden unreality
As you in your neglect of their performance,—
Though for their season we must humor them
For what they are: devils undoubtedly,
But not so parlous and implacable
In their undoing of poor human triumph
As easy fashion—or brief novelty
That ails even while it grows, and like sick fruit
Falls down anon to an indifferent earth
To break with inward rot. I say all this,
And I concede, in honor of your silence,
A waste of innocent facility
In tints of other colors than are mine.
I cannot paint with words, but there's a time
For most of us when words are all we have
To serve our stricken souls. And here you say,
"Be careful, or you may commit your soul
Soon to the very devil of your denial."
I might have wagered on you to say that,
Knowing that I believe in you too surely
To spoil you with a kick or paint you over.

No, my good friend, Mynheer Rembrandt van Ryn—
Sometime a personage in Amsterdam,
But now not much—I shall not give myself
To be the sport of any dragon-spawn
Of Holland, or elsewhere. Holland was hell
Not long ago, and there were dragons then
More to be fought than any of these we see
That we may foster now. They are not real,
But not for that the less to be regarded;
For there are slimy tyrants born of nothing
That harden slowly into seeming life
And have the strength of madness. I confess,
Accordingly, the wisdom of your care
That I look out for them. Whether I would
Or not, I must; and here we are as one
With our necessity. For though you loom
A little harsh in your respect of time
And circumstance, and of ordained eclipse,
We know together of a golden flood
That with its overflow shall drown away
The dikes that held it; and we know thereby
That in its rising light there lives a fire
No devils that are lodging here in Holland
Shall put out wholly, or much agitate,
Except in unofficial preparation
They put out first the sun. It's well enough
To think of them; wherefore I thank you, sir,
Alike for your remembrance and attention.

But there are demons that are longer-lived
Than doubts that have a brief and evil term
To congregate among the futile shards
And architraves of eminent collapse.
They are a many-favored family,
All told, with not a misbegotten dwarf
Among the rest that I can love so little
As one occult abortion in especial
Who perches on a picture (when it's done)
And says, "What of it, Rembrandt, if you do?"
This incubus would seem to be a sort
Of chorus, indicating, for our good,
The silence of the few friends that are left:
"What of it, Rembrandt, even if you know?"
It says again; "and you don't know for certain.
What if in fifty or a hundred years
They find you out? You may have gone meanwhile
So greatly to the dogs that you'll not care
Much what they find. If this be all you are—
This unaccountable aspiring insect—
You'll sleep as easy in oblivion
As any sacred monk or parricide;
And if, as you conceive, you are eternal,
Your soul may laugh, remembering (if a soul
Remembers) your befrenzied aspiration
To smear with certain ochres and some oil
A few more perishable ells of cloth,
And once or twice, to square your vanity,
Prove it was you alone that should achieve
A mortal eye—that may, no less, tomorrow
Show an immortal reason why today

Men see no more. And what's a mortal eye
More than a mortal herring, who has eyes
As well as you? Why not paint herrings, Rembrandt?
Or if not herrings, why not a split beef?
Perceive it only in its unalloyed
Integrity, and you may find in it
A beautified accomplishment no less
Indigenous than one that appertains
To gentlemen and ladies eating it.
The same God planned and made you, beef and human;
And one, but for His whim, might be the other."

That's how he says it, Rembrandt, if you listen;
He says it, and he goes. And then, sometimes,
There comes another spirit in his place—
One with a more engaging argument,
And with a softer note for saying truth
Not soft. Whether it be the truth or not,
I name it so; for there's a string in me
Somewhere that answers—which is natural,
Since I am but a living instrument
Played on by powers that are invisible.
"You might go faster, if not quite so far,"
He says, "if in your vexed economy
There lived a faculty for saying yes
And meaning no, and then for doing neither;
But since Apollo sees it otherwise,
Your Dutchmen, who are swearing at you still
For your pernicious filching of their florins,
May likely curse you down their generation,
Not having understood there was no malice
Or grinning evil in a golden shadow
That shall outshine their slight identities
And hold their faces when their names are nothing.

But this, as you discern, or should by now
Surmise, for you is neither here nor there:
You made your picture as your demon willed it;
That's about all of that. Now make as many
As may be to be made,—for so you will,
Whatever the toll may be, and hold your light
So that you see, without so much to blind you
As even the cobweb-flash of a misgiving,
Assured and certain that if you see right
Others will have to see—albeit their seeing
Shall irk them out of their serenity
For such a time as umbrage may require.
But there are many reptiles in the night
That now is coming on, and they are hungry;
And there's a Rembrandt to be satisfied
Who never will be, howsoever much
He be assured of an ascendency
That has not yet a shadow's worth of sound
Where Holland has its ears. And what of that?
Have you the weary leisure or sick wit
That breeds of its indifference a false envy
That is the vermin on accomplishment?
Are you inaugurating your new service
With fasting for a food you would not eat?
You are the servant, Rembrandt, not the master,—
But you are not assigned with other slaves
That in their freedom are the most in fear.
One of the few that are so fortunate
As to be told their task and to be given
A skill to do it with a tool too keen
For timid safety, bow your elected head
Under the stars tonight, and whip your devils
Each to his nest in hell. Forget your days,
And so forgive the years that may not be

So many as to be more than you may need
For your particular consistency
In your peculiar folly. You are counting
Some fewer years than forty at your heels;
And they have not pursued your gait so fast
As your oblivion—which has beaten them,
And rides now on your neck like an old man
With iron shins and fingers. Let him ride
(You haven't so much to say now about that),
And in a proper season let him run.
You may be dead then, even as you may now
Anticipate some other mortal strokes
Attending your felicity; and for that,
Oblivion heretofore has done some running
Away from graves, and will do more of it."

That's how it is your wiser spirit speaks,
Rembrandt. If you believe him, why complain?
If not, why paint? And why, in any event,
Look back for the old joy and the old roses,
Or the old fame? They are all gone together,
And Saskia with them; and with her left out,
They would avail no more now than one strand
Of Samson's hair wound round his little finger
Before the temple fell. Nor more are you
In any sudden danger to forget
That in Apollo's house there are no clocks
Or calendars to say for you in time
How far you are away from Amsterdam,
Or that the one same law that bids you see
Where now you see alone forbids in turn
Your light from Holland eyes till Holland ears
Are told of it; for that way, my good fellow,
Is one way more to death. If at the first

Of your long turning, which may still be longer
Than even your faith has measured it, you sigh
For distant welcome that may not be seen,
Or wayside shouting that will not be heard,
You may as well accommodate your greatness
To the convenience of an easy ditch,
And, anchored there with all your widowed gold,
Forget your darkness in the dark, and hear
No longer the cold wash of Holland scorn.

From

DIONYSUS IN DOUBT

HAUNTED HOUSE

Here was a place where none would ever come
For shelter, save as we did from the rain.
We saw no ghost, yet once outside again
Each wondered why the other should be dumb;
For we had fronted nothing worse than gloom
And ruin, and to our vision it was plain
Where thrift, outshivering fear, had let remain
Some chairs that were like skeletons of home.

There were no trackless footsteps on the floor
Above us, and there were no sounds elsewhere.
But there was more than sound; and there was more
Than just an axe that once was in the air
Between us and the chimney, long before
Our time. So townsmen said who found her there.

THE SHEAVES

Where long the shadows of the wind had rolled,
Green wheat was yielding to the change assigned;
And as by some vast magic undivined
The world was turning slowly into gold.
Like nothing that was ever bought or sold
It waited there, the body and the mind;
And with a mighty meaning of a kind
That tells the more the more it is not told.

So in a land where all days are not fair,
Fair days went on till on another day
A thousand golden sheaves were lying there,
Shining and still, but not for long to stay—
As if a thousand girls with golden hair
Might rise from where they slept and go away.

KARMA

Christmas was in the air and all was well
With him, but for a few confusing flaws
In divers of God's images. Because
A friend of his would neither buy nor sell,
Was he to answer for the axe that fell?
He pondered; and the reason for it was,
Partly, a slowly freezing Santa Claus
Upon the corner, with his beard and bell.

Acknowledging an improvident surprise,
He magnified a fancy that he wished
The friend whom he had wrecked were here again.
Not sure of that, he found a compromise;
And from the fulness of his heart he fished
A dime for Jesus who had died for men.

As It Looked Then

In a sick shade of spruce, moss-webbed, rock-fed,
Where, long unfollowed by sagacious man,
A scrub that once had been a pathway ran
Blindly from nowhere and to nowhere led,
One might as well have been among the dead
As half way there alive; so I began
Like a malingering pioneer to plan
A vain return—with one last look ahead.

And it was then that like a spoken word
Where there was none to speak, insensibly
A flash of blue that might have been a bird
Grew soon to the calm wonder of the sea—
Calm as a quiet sky that looked to be
Arching a world where nothing had occurred.

A MAN IN OUR TOWN

We pitied him as one too much at ease
With Nemesis and impending indigence;
Also, as if by way of recompense,
We sought him always in extremities;
And while ways more like ours had more to please
Our common code than his improvidence,
There lurked alive in our experience
His homely genius for emergencies.

He was not one for men to marvel at,
And yet there was another neighborhood
When he was gone, and many a thrifty tear.
There was an increase in a man like that;
And though he be forgotten, it was good
For more than one of you that he was here.

WHY HE WAS THERE

Much as he left it when he went from us
Here was the room again where he had been
So long that something of him should be seen,
Or felt—and so it was. Incredulous,
I turned about, loath to be greeted thus,
And there he was in his old chair, serene
As ever, and as laconic and as lean
As when he lived, and as cadaverous.

Calm as he was of old when we were young,
He sat there gazing at the pallid flame
Before him. "And how far will this go on?"
I thought. He felt the failure of my tongue,
And smiled: "I was not here until you came;
And I shall not be here when you are gone."

NEW ENGLAND

Here where the wind is always north-north-east
And children learn to walk on frozen toes,
Wonder begets an envy of all those
Who boil elsewhere with such a lyric yeast
Of love that you will hear them at a feast
Where demons would appeal for some repose,
Still clamoring where the chalice overflows
And crying wildest who have drunk the least.

Passion is here a soilure of the wits,
We're told, and Love a cross for them to bear;
Joy shivers in the corner where she knits
And Conscience always has the rocking-chair,
Cheerful as when she tortured into fits
The first cat that was ever killed by Care.

REUNION

By some derision of wild circumstance
Not then our pleasure somehow to perceive,
Last night we fell together to achieve
A light eclipse of years. But the pale chance
Of youth resumed was lost. Time gave a glance
At each of us, and there was no reprieve;
And when there was at last a way to leave,
Farewell was a foreseen extravagance.

Tonight the west has yet a failing red,
While silence whispers of all things not here;
And round there where the fire was that is dead,
Dusk-hidden tenants that are chairs appear.
The same old stars will soon be overhead,
But not so friendly and not quite so near.

A CHRISTMAS SONNET

For One in Doubt

While you that in your sorrow disavow
Service and hope, see love and brotherhood
Far off as ever, it will do no good
For you to wear his thorns upon your brow
For doubt of him. And should you question how
To serve him best, he might say, if he could,
"Whether or not the cross was made of wood
Whereon you nailed me, is no matter now."

Though other saviors have in older lore
A Legend, and for older gods have died—
Though death may wear the crown it always wore
And ignorance be still the sword of pride—
Something is here that was not here before,
And strangely has not yet been crucified.

APPENDICES

ONE

ROBINSON SPEAKING

Robinson was a very private and reticent man; he never taught or lectured or gave readings or interviews. These various comments on life and the art of poetry come for the most part from letters and the memoirs of friends.

Many causes prevent poetry from being correctly appraised in its own time. Any poetry that is marked by violence, that is conspicuous in color, that is sensationally odd, makes an immediate appeal. On the other hand, poetry that is not noticeably eccentric sometimes fails for years to attract any attention. . . . More than ever before, oddity and violence are bringing into prominence poets who have little besides these two qualities to offer the world. . . .

Nobody devoted as much as an inch to me. I did not exist.

I know that many of the new writers insist that it is harder to write good *vers libre* than to write good rhymed poetry. And judging from some of their results, I am inclined to agree with them.

I have only one objection to free verse and that is that it seems to me to be a makeshift. About the best I can say is that the best free verse that I have seen contains subject matter for good poems.

[*Asked if he himself ever wrote free verse*] No, I write badly enough as it is.

I had no idea of establishing any new movement in poetry. As I look back I see that I wrote as I did without considering how much of the old poetical machinery I left behind. I see now that I have always disliked inversions as well as many other conventional solemnities which seem to have had their day. I could never, even as a child, see any good reason why the language of verse should be distorted almost out of recognition in order to be poetical.

I am essentially a classicist in poetic composition, and I believe that the accepted media for the masters of the past will continue to be used in the future. There is, of course, room for infinite variety, manipulation and invention within the limits of traditional forms and meters, but any violent deviation from the classic mean may be a confession of inability to do the real thing, poetically speaking.

My poetry is rat poison to editors, but here and there a Philistine seems to like it.

I also make free to say that many of my verses were written with a conscious hope that they might make some despairing devil a little stronger and a little better satisfied with things— not as they are, but as they are to be.

Nine-tenths of poetry is *how* it's done. . . . Ideas are, of course, inseparable from the medium, but much memorable poetry is not important for what is said.

As far as I can make out, poetry is a sort of secretion.

When a man puts by fiction and poetry—especially poetry— he is unconsciously brutalizing himself.

I should not say there was any philosophy in my poetry beyond an instinctive protest against a materialist conception of life.

I've always rather liked the queer, odd sticks of men, that's all.

[*Re Miniver Cheevy and Eben Flood*]. . . . sustained by dreams and soothed by drink. I certainly should know them. I'm one of them.

[*Re his youthful poem to Whitman*] I was very young when I wrote it, but I knew all the time I was writing it that I didn't really mean it. . . . Whitman seems greater than he is. . . . I may be wrong; I probably am. But I have never been able to find so much in him.

I think we must leave my contemporaries out of it. I don't mind your saying, though, that I think a lot of Robert Frost's work.

Sociology—whatever the word means—usually kills poetry, art of any kind.

People ask me why I do not do the short poems any more. I can't. They don't come any more. . . . Just now they are all busy telling me that I ought not to be writing these long poems. Maybe not. But how can anybody know—anybody except myself? They happen to be the thing that's in my blood; so I've got to write them.

[*Asked why he endured so many years of poverty*] Because I am a faithful servant of Apollo.

I was born with my skin inside out.

I am just beginning fully to realize that America is the hopper through which the whole civilization of the world is to be ground—consciously or otherwise. I am not much of an American, either—in a popular way; but I am glad to feel an inkling as to what the western continent was made for.

The thing that astonished me was that the President of the United States should be able to find the time to dig up a young poet out of the rather dark obscurity that veiled him from view and to think of ways to help. It wasn't so astonishing that he should be *disposed* to help. He was that kind of man. There were depths in his nature which, during his lifetime, he was not too often credited with.

[*Re the Custom House job*] It is the third offer that has come my way through Roosevelt's influence. I had a note from him regarding this one that was short and to the point: "Good salary. Little work. Soft snap!"

[*Re the following passage from Proust: "All that we can say is that everything is arranged in this life as though we entered it carrying the burden of obligations contracted in a former life; there is no reason inherent in the conditions of life on this earth that can make us consider ourselves obliged to do good, to be fastidious, to be polite even, nor make the talented artist consider himself obliged to begin over again a score of times a piece of work the admiration aroused by which will matter little to his body devoured by worms, like the patch of yellow wall painted with so much knowledge and skill by an artist who must for ever remain unknown and is barely identified under the name Vermeer. All these obligations which have not their sanction in our present life seem to belong to a different world, founded upon kindness, scrupulosity, self-sacrifice, a world entirely different from this, which we leave in order to be born into this world, before perhaps returning to live under the sway of those unknown laws which we have obeyed because we bore their precepts in our hearts, knowing not whose hand had traced them there—those laws to which every profound work of the intellect brings us nearer and which are invisible only—and still!—to fools."*] That comes nearer to being one hundred per cent true than anything I have heard in a long time.

The willingness "to be a child again" comes hard—so hard that it will never come to many who are in the world today. That is not what they are here for.

The great art of life is to suffer without worrying.

I could never have done *anything* but write poetry.

TWO

COMMENTARY BY SCHOLARS, CRITICS, AND OTHER POETS

The trouble in Robinson's life was mostly interior. Some force of repression, not exactly unknown to New England character, had locked up his powers for living by, or articulating openly, the feelings his poems show him to have had. Even in the poems themselves a direct release of passion or desire is infrequent; they "contain," or emerge out of, enormous depths of feeling, but it is a feeling pressed into oblique irony or disciplined into austere reflection. He was not the man to yield himself to what Henry James once called "promiscuous revelation."

Thinking of such poems [*as Eros Turannos*] and trying to understand how it is that in their plainness they can seem so magnificent, one finds oneself falling back on terms like "sincerity" and "honesty." They are terms notoriously inadequate and tricky, yet inescapable in discussing poets like Robinson and Thomas Hardy. It is not, after all, as if one wants to say about more brilliant poets like Eliot and Yeats that they are insincere or lacking in honesty; of course not. What one does want to suggest is that in poems like Robinson's "Eros Turannos" and "Hillcrest," as in Hardy's "The Going" and "At Castle Boterel," there is an abandonment of all pretense and pose, all protectiveness and persona. At such moments the poet seems beyond decoration and defense; he leaves himself vulnerable, open to the pain of his self; he cares nothing for consolation; he looks at defeat and does not blink. It is a literature beyond the literary.

—IRVING HOWE

Robinson was never so romantically disillusioned that he could be for long disturbed over the discrepancy between actual and ideal, illusion and reality; for him, the real irony, the comedy, lay in man's wilful misconception of life and his role in it. . . . In "Veteran Sirens" all the terrible irony of mankind's wilful refusal to face facts emerges in the pitying portrait of superannuated whores. . . . And we are all life's whores. What strikes Robinson as ironic is not the old discrepancy between illusion and reality, not the wastage of time, but the supreme dissipation of the expense of spirit in a waste of shame, folly and deceit. The stern, still-Calvinist view of carnal sin here has become a trope for life, for the way we all bargain with life for a living and are finally cheated.

Much of what Robinson has to say here [*Hillcrest*] some readers are bound to dislike; it is not fashionable to contemplate one's "ruins and regrets" nor to see childhood as something other than perfection, nor will many readers ever attune themselves to such statements as the poem explicitly makes as well as implicitly signifies. Stoicism has a poor reputation, but it is a Roman virtue and Robinson is a Roman among barbarians.

It cannot be coincidence entirely that the first work he did in poetry was a translation of Virgil; both poets were candidly "derivative" and yet unmistakably themselves. Both were at home in town and country: *Rus in urbe, urbs in rure.* To each poet, for all he may have dealt with the forlorn and the tragic, life was good if only it pointed beyond itself. They are poets of the civilized heart and mind, whom no one and nothing can shock, surprise or embitter.

—Louis Coxe

I have had to tell a number of people in my day what I thought of their writing. You are one of the few I have wanted to tell—one of the very few. Now I have my chance to tell you. I have had some sort of real satisfaction in everything of yours I have read. I hope I make that sweeping enough.

—Robert Frost

Robinson's techniques were more or less the same as those of his contemporaries, the meters strict always, so strict and even jingly at times as to suggest light verse. Only—and this makes all the difference—the pieties are not quite in place. . . .

The Torrent and the Night Before is the first sign in verse of the stirring of some new thing already felt in certain recent novels and stories. Once Robinson had opened the package of small blue-backed books he had paid fifty-two dollars to have printed, once he had begun to address the three hundred and twelve copies to the lucky recipients he had chosen, he was— he had become—the first modern American poet. This debut is less famous than Whitman's, and certainly less revolutionary, but it will do, and what fame it bears is not misplaced. The work in it is surprisingly mature, even the poems that go wrong, as most of them predictably do. Still, four or five small masterpieces are here to be discovered, poems that even before the century turned had become anthology pieces and would remain so ever after. . . .

—Donald Justice

Surely there is enough common ground between Hawthorne and Robinson—the caution and reserve, the austere contemplation of failure, the concentration on psychology, the inordinate love of melodrama, the highly developed "historical sense" that intermittently blends and compares the past and present—to suggest that Hawthorne was a major source for Robinson's production. Remembering the significant and deep-seated spiritual opposition of Emerson and Hawthorne, the critic might naturally look here for one of the sources of that sturdy realism in spiritual matters that marks Robinson's poetry and that limits and controls the influence of Emerson.

Wit, generally suppressed in English poetry for more than a century, returned in Robinson's poetry, together with irony and a sterner intellectual discipline. His contribution to the purification of poetic language was equally substantial: ridding his verse of the stilted romantic diction that had been accreting since the early nineteenth century, he turned instead to a conversational and argumentative manner, reintroduced the language of genuine erudition, and provided poetry with a medium that had power and resiliency and was capable of intellectual distinctions. All these qualities were to prove of central importance in the later development of twentieth-century poetry, although most critics continue to be unconscious of Robinson's contribution to this development.

Taking Robinson's career as a whole, I am tempted to say that it implies a nearly total antithesis of all that Whitman had called for in American art.

—EDWIN S. FUSSELL

He is a slow and patient poet; taking his time to say a thing as he wishes to say it is one of his fundamental qualities. This has worked against him, particularly since his work has survived into an age of anything but slow and patient readers. The

pedestrian movement of much of his work has made him un-
popular in an era when the piling on of startling effects, the
cramming of the poetic line with all the spoils it can carry, is
regarded not so much as a criterion of good or superior verse
of a certain kind, but as poetry itself, other kinds being rele-
gated to inferior categories yet to be named.

One is held by the curious dry magic that seems so eminently
unmagical, that bears no resemblance to the elfin or purely
verbal or native-woodnote magic for which English verse is
justly celebrated. It is a magic for which there is very little
precedent in all literature.

In creating a body of major poetry with devices usually
thought to be unfruitful for the creative act—irresolution, ab-
straction, conjecture, a dry, nearly imageless mode of address
that tends always toward the general without ever supplying
the resolving judgment that we expect of generalization—
Robinson has done what good poets have always done: by
means of his "cumulative silences" as well as by his actual
lines, he has forced us to reexamine and finally to redefine
what poetry is—or our notion of it—and so has enabled po-
etry to include more, to *be* more, than it was before he wrote.

—James Dickey

His lyric perceptions, like his human values, are rooted in the
known and the possible—the capacities of man which survive
even in his sorriest condition of stultification and confusion.
He never allowed his tragic sense to carry him toward the im-
potent Promethean rhetoric of Jeffers. It is these firm roots,
not only in experience but in language, that bind Robinson so
certainly to his moment in modern history—to its economic

and social conditions, its moral conflict, its political crisis and immense human claims. He is a realist not only in conscience but in style and diction; in *milieu* as much as in imagery; and this gives him his license to explore the problems of abstract casuistry and moral contradiction which he filed down into that style of attenuated rumination, impassioned hair-splitting, and bleak aphorism which always remain unmistakably his own.

He was a poet without school or cenacle; he was fundamentally as inimitable as unapproachable; and his bleaker or more repetitious volumes might almost be interpreted as a warning to the public to expect from him none of the innovation or sensationalism that makes literary creeds, movements, and manifestoes. For this he was scorned by youthful insurgents, and apparently by most of the greater names that rival his in recent literature. His influence was more subtle. He brought form and toughness of language into modern verse long before most of his contemporaries, and he corrected by modest example a slow drift toward slovenly habits and facile impressionism in poetic thought.

—Morton Dauwen Zabel

We must bring Robinson back. Although he remains among the best American poets, Robinson now goes largely unread. An insidious form of neglect enshrines one minor effort, genuflects, and bypasses the best work.... We must restore Robinson to the American pantheon.

—Donald Hall

... nearly all of Robinson's best poems appear to deal with particular persons and situations; in these poems his examination is careful and intelligent, his method is analytic, and his style is mainly very distinguished. If we are to risk pushing historical influences for all they are worth, we may say that in such poems Robinson exhibits the New England taste for practical morality, a passionate curiosity about individual dramas, and that in examining them he is guided by the moral and spiritual values of the general Christian tradition as they have come down to him in the form of folk wisdom or common sense, although in the application of these values he shows a penetration and subtlety which are the measure of his genius.

. . . he became on certain occasions one of the most remarkable poets in our language. His style at its best is as free from the provincialism of time and of place as the best writing of Jonson and Herbert. This impersonal greatness of style has been seldom achieved in the twentieth century.

—YVOR WINTERS

THREE

Robert Frost's Introduction to E. A. Robinson's *King Jasper*

It may come to the notice of posterity (and then again it may not) that this, our age, ran wild in the quest of new ways to be new. The one old way to be new no longer served. Science put it into our heads that there must be new ways to be new. Those tried were largely by subtraction—elimination. Poetry, for example, was tried without punctuation. It was tried without capital letters. It was tried without metric frame on which to measure the rhythm. It was tried without any images but those to the eye; and a loud general intoning had to be kept up to cover the total loss of specific images to the ear, those dramatic tones of voice which had hitherto constituted the better half of poetry. It was tried without content under the trade name of poesie pure. It was tried without phrase, epigram, coherence, logic and consistency. It was tried without ability. I took the confession of one who had had deliberately to unlearn what he knew. He made a back-pedalling movement of his hands to illustrate the process. It was tried premature like the delicacy of unborn calf in Asia. It was tried without feeling or sentiment like murder for small pay in the underworld. These many things was it tried without, and what had we left?

Still something. The limits of poetry had been sorely strained, but the hope was that the idea had been somewhat brought out.

Robinson stayed content with the old-fashioned way to be new. I remember bringing the subject up with him. How does a man come on his difference, and how does he feel about it when he first finds it out? At first it may well frighten him, as his difference with the Church frightened Martin Luther. There is such a thing as being too willing to be different. And what shall we say to people who are not only willing but anxious? What assurance have they that their difference is not insane, eccentric, abortive, unintelligible? Two fears should follow us through life. There is the fear that we shan't prove worthy in the eyes of someone who knows us at least as well as we know ourselves. That is the fear of God. And there is the fear of Man—the fear that men won't understand us and we shall be cut off from them.

We began in infancy by establishing correspondence of eyes with eyes. We recognized that they were the same feature and we could do the same things with them. We went on to the visible motion of the lips—smile answered smile; then cautiously, by trial and error, to compare the invisible muscles of the mouth and throat. They were the same and could make the same sounds. We were still together. So far, so good. From here on the wonder grows. It has been said that recognition in art is all. Better say correspondence is all. Mind must convince mind that it can uncurl and wave the same filaments of subtlety, soul convince soul that it can give off the same shimmers of eternity. At no point would anyone but a brute fool want to break off this correspondence. It is all there is to satisfaction; and it is salutary to live in the fear of its being broken off.

The latest proposed experiment of the experimentalists is to use poetry as a vehicle of grievances against the un-

Utopian state. As I say, most of their experiments have been by subtraction. This would be by addition of an ingredient that latter-day poetry has lacked. A distinction must be made between griefs and grievances. Grievances are probably more useful than griefs. I read in a sort of Sunday School leaflet from Moscow that the grievances of Chekhov against the sordidness and dullness of his home-town society have done away with the sordidness and dullness of home-town society all over Russia. They were celebrating the event. The grievances of the great Russians of the last century have given Russia a revolution. The grievances of their great followers in America may well give us, if not a revolution, at least some palliative pensions. We must suffer them to put life at its ugliest and forbid them not as we value our reputation for liberality.

I had it from one of the youngest lately: "Whereas we once thought literature should be without content, we now know it should be charged full of propaganda." Wrong twice, I told him. Wrong twice and of theory prepense. But he returned to his position after a moment out for reassembly: "Surely art can be considered good only as it prompts to action." How soon, I asked him. But there is danger of undue levity in teasing the young. The experiment is evidently started. Grievances are certainly a power and are going to be turned on. We must be very tender of our dreamers. They may seem like picketers or members of the committee on rules for the moment. We shan't mind what they seem, if only they produce real poems.

But for me, I don't like grievances. I find I gently let them alone wherever published. What I like is griefs and I like them Robinsonianly profound. I suppose there is no use in asking, but I should think we might be indulged to the extent of having grievances restricted to prose if prose will accept the imposition, and leaving poetry free to go its way in tears.

Robinson was a prince of heartachers amid countless achers of another part. The sincerity he wrought in was all sad. He asserted the sacred right of poetry to lean its breast to a thorn and sing its dolefullest. Let weasels suck eggs. I know better where to look for melancholy. A few superficial irritable grievances, perhaps, as was only human, but these are forgotten in the depth of griefs to which he plunged us.

Grievances are a form of impatience. Griefs are a form of patience. We may be required by law to throw away patience as we have been required to surrender gold; since by throwing away patience and joining the impatient in one last rush on the citadel of evil, the hope is we may end the need of patience. There will be nothing left to be patient about. The day of perfection waits on unanimous social action. Two or three more good national elections should do the business. It has been similarly urged on us to give up courage, make cowardice a virtue, and see if that won't end war, and the need of courage. Desert religion for science, clean out the holes and corners of the residual unknown, and there will be no more need of religion. (Religion is merely consolation for what we don't know.) But suppose there was some mistake; and the evil stood siege, the war didn't end, and something remained unknowable. Our having disarmed would make our case worse than it had ever been before. Nothing in the latest advices from Wall Street, the League of Nations, or the Vatican inclines me to give up my holdings in patient grief.

There were Robinson and I, it was years ago, and the place (near Boston Common) was the Place, as we liked afterward to call it, of Bitters, because it was with bitters, though without bitterness, we could sit there and look out on the welter of dissatisfaction and experiment in the world around us. It was too long ago to remember who said what, but the sense of the meeting was, we didn't care how arrant a reformer or experimentalist a man was if he gave us real poems. For ourselves, we would hate to be read for any theory upon which we might be supposed to write. We doubted any poem could persist for any theory upon which it might have been written. Take the theory that poetry in our language could be treated as quantitative, for example. Poems had been written in spite of it. And poems are all that matter. The utmost of ambition is to lodge a few poems where they will be hard to get rid of, to lodge a few irreducible bits where Robinson lodged more than his share.

For forty years it was phrase on phrase on phrase with Robinson and every one the closest delineation of something that *is* something. Any poet, to resemble him in the least, would have to resemble him in that grazing closeness to the spiritual realities. If books of verse were to be indexed by lines first in importance instead of lines first in position, many of Robinson's poems would be represented several times over. This should be seen to. The only possible objection is that it could not be done by any mere hireling of the moment, but would have to be the work of someone who had taken his impressions freely before he had any notion of their use. A particular poem's being represented several times would only increase the chance of its being located.

The first poet I ever sat down with to talk about poetry was Ezra Pound. It was in London in 1913. The first poet we talked about, to the best of my recollection, was Edwin Arlington Robinson. I was fresh from America and having read *The Town Down the River*. Beginning at that book I have slowly spread my reading of Robinson twenty years backward and forward, about equally in both directions.

I remember the pleasure with which Pound and I laughed over the fourth "thought" in

> Miniver thought and thought and thought
> And thought about it.

Three "thoughts" would have been "adequate" as the critical praise-word then was. There would have been nothing to complain of if it had been left at three. The fourth made the intolerable touch of poetry. With the fourth the fun began. I was taken out on the strength of our community of opinion here to be rewarded with an introduction to Miss May Sinclair, who had qualified as the patron authority on young and new poets by the sympathy she had shown them in *The Divine Fire.*

There is more to it than the number of the "thoughts." There is the way the last one turns up by surprise round the corner, the way the shape of the stanza is played with, the easy way the obstacle of verse is turned to advantage. The mischief is in it.

> One pauses half afraid
> To say for certain that he played—

a man as sorrowful as Robinson. His death was sad to those who knew him, but nowhere near as sad as the lifetime of poetry to which he attuned our ears. Nevertheless, I say his much-admired restraint lies wholly in his never having let grief go further than it could in play. So far shall grief go, so far shall philosophy go, so far shall confidences go, and no further. Taste may set the limit. Humor is a surer dependence.

> Once a man was there all night
> Expecting something every minute.

I know what the man wanted of Old King Cole. He wanted the heart out of his mystery. He was the friend who stands at the end of a poem ready in waiting to catch you by both hands with enthusiasm and drag you off your balance over the last punctuation mark into more than you meant to say. "I under-

stand the poem all right, but please tell me what is behind it."
Such presumption needs to be twinkled at and baffled. The
answer must be, "If I had wanted you to know, I should have
told you in the poem."

We early have Robinson's word for it:

> The games we play
> To fill the frittered minutes of a day
> Good glasses are to read the spirit through.

He speaks somewhere of Crabbe's stubborn skill. His own
was a happy skill. His theme was unhappiness itself, but his
skill was as happy as it was playful. There is that comforting
thought for those who suffered to see him suffer. Let it be said
at the risk of offending the humorless in poetry's train (for
there are a few such): his art was more than playful; it was hu-
morous.

The style is the man. Rather say the style is the way the
man takes himself; and to be at all charming or even bearable,
the way is almost rigidly prescribed. If it is with outer seri-
ousness, it must be with inner humor. If it is with outer humor,
it must be with inner seriousness. Neither one alone without
the other under it will do. Robinson was thinking as much in
his sonnet on Tom Hood. One ordeal of Mark Twain was the
constant fear that his occluded seriousness would be over-
looked. That betrayed him into his two or three books of out-
and-out seriousness.

Miniver Cheevy was long ago. The glint I mean has kept
coming to the surface of the fabric all down the years. Yes-
terday in conversation, I was using "The Mill." Robinson
could make lyric talk like drama. What imagination for
speech in "John Gorham"! He is at his height between quota-
tion marks.

> The miller's wife had waited long.
> The tea was cold, the fire was dead.
> And there might yet be nothing wrong
> In how he went and what he said.
> "There are no millers any more,"
> Was all that she had heard him say.

"There are no millers any more." It might be an edict of the New Deal against processors (as we now dignify them). But no, it is of wider application. It is a sinister jest at the expense of all investors of life or capital. The market shifts and leaves them with a car-barn full of dead trolley cars. At twenty I commit myself to a life of religion. Now, if religion should go out of fashion in twenty-five years, there would I be, forty-five years old, unfitted for anything else and too old to learn anything else. It seems immoral to have to bet on such high things as lives of art, business, or the church. But in effect, we have no alternative. None but an all-wise and all-powerful government could take the responsibility of keeping us out of gambling or of insuring us against loss once we were in.

The guarded pathos of "Mr. Flood's Party" is what makes it merciless. We are to bear in mind the number of moons listening. Two, as on the planet Mars. No less. No more ("No more, sir, that's enough"). One moon (albeit a moon, no sun) would have laid grief too bare. More than two would have dissipated grief entirely and would have amounted to dissipation. The emotion had to be held at a point.

> He set the jug down slowly at his feet
> With trembling care, knowing that most things break,
> And only when assured that on firm earth
> It stood, as the uncertain lives of men
> Assuredly did not—

There twice it gleams. Nor is it lost even where it is perhaps lost sight of in the dazzle of all those golden girls at the end of "The Sheaves." Granted a few fair days in a world where not all days are fair.

> "Well, Mr. Flood, we have the harvest moon
> Again, and we may not have many more.
> The bird is on the wing, the poet says,
> And you and I have said it here before.
> Drink to the bird."

Poetry transcends itself in the playfulness of the toast.

Robinson has gone to his place in American literature and left his human place among us vacant. We mourn, but with the qualification that after all, his life was a revel in the felicities of language. And not just to no purpose. None could deplore,

> The inscrutable profusion of the Lord
> Who shaped as one of us a thing

so sad and at the same time so happy in achievement. Not for me to search his sadness to its source. He knew how to forbid encroachment. And there is solid satisfaction in a sadness that is not just a fishing for ministration and consolation. Give us immedicable woes—woes that nothing can be done for—woes flat and final. And then to play. The play's the thing. Play's the thing. All virtue in "as if."

> As if the last of days
> Were fading and all wars were done.

As if they were. As if, as if!

NOTES

Luke Havergal   This is one of the poems that President Roosevelt was particularly moved by, although he confessed that he did not understand it, and indeed many good readers have found it mysterious. Yvor Winters says that Luke is addressed by his dead lover, which may well be the case; but since the voice of the poem speaks in both the first and third persons, I wonder if there might not be a third character, perhaps the other man in a love triangle, who is luring Luke Havergal to join the woman in death. (To go west is to die.) As in "Cortège" and "Late Summer" and in many other poems, a love triangle, especially a tortured one, is one of the poet's obsessive subjects.

The House on the Hill   Robinson's first mentor, Dr. Alanson Tucker Schumann, was very fond of the intricate French forms, and the local poetry circle wrote a good many of them. Robinson's other ballades and villanelles, written in his teens, are not very successful, although wonderfully accomplished for a boy; this villanelle in trimeters is, to my mind, one of the best in English.

Zola   Émile Zola, 1840–1902, French novelist and critic whose dark, naturalistic novels are unsparing depictions of the lower depths. Robinson probably had not at this time read much of his work; Zola might well have questioned "the human heart / of God" or "the divine heart of man" as more Robinsonian than Zolaesque.

The Clerks It was thought for a long time that Robinson had in mind an old store in Gardiner—Cusick & Lincoln—that sold boots and shoes, but had made it a dry goods store because he liked the rare word *alnage,* a variant of *aulnage,* which is a measure of cloth. But from 1862 to 1884, J. T. Stone's Dry Goods occupied that building; when Cusick and Lincoln opened for business, J. T. Stone moved next door. Robinson would have shopped at both stores and known the clerks well. (I owe this revelation to Joanne D. Clark of Gardiner.)

Thomas Hood Hood, 1799–1845, is best known for "The Bridge of Sighs" but most of his work consists of punning comical and topical verse. His humor and spirit are remarkable in a man long exhausted by consumption and dogged by poverty and debt. I am indebted to John Hollander for the identification of *the branded man of Lynn* and of *Ines.* The branded man (not literally Hood's brother) is the protagonist of Hood's poem, "The Dream of Eugene Aram," an intellectual murderer whose crime, long undetected, is eventually revealed. The poem ends:

> Two stern-faced men set out from Lynn,
> Through the cold and heavy mist;
> And Eugene Aram walked between,
> With gyves upon his wrist.

Hood also wrote a poem called "Fair Ines," which begins

> O saw ye not fair Ines?
> She's gone into the west,
> To dazzle when the sun is down,
> And rob the world of rest.

Horace to Leuconoë A fairly accurate translation of Horace's Ode, I, 11, a poem translated many times over the centuries by such poets as C. S. Calverly, Rudyard Kipling, Ezra Pound, and David Ferry (and the source of the famous phrase, *carpe diem*). Kipling's very free version is undoubtedly the shortest:

Lucy, do not look ahead: We shall be a long time dead.
Take whatever you can see: And, incidentally, take me.

The *Chaldeans* and Babylonians were so obsessed with astrology and other occult methods of seeing into the future that the word *Chaldean* came to mean an astrologer or fortune-teller (and is so used in the Bible). Robinson's Italian sonnet may well be the most beautiful version in English, but it would be very hard to improve on what David Ferry has done with the last few lines:

The time we have is short.
  Cut short your hopes for longer.
Now as I say these words,
  Time has already fled
Backwards away—
  Leuconoë—
    Hold on to the day.

George Crabbe   George Crabbe, 1754–1832, was a master of the plain style who wrote several long poems in heroic couplets, including "The Village" and "The Parish Register," in which he demolished Goldsmith's idealized pastoral by describing with great accuracy and sympathy the squalor and blighted promises, as well as the mirth and eccentricities, of the poor folk of his native town. Probably his best known poem is the excellent and compelling "Peter Grimes," on which Benjamin Britten based his opera.

Verlaine   Paul Verlaine, 1844–1896, French symbolist poet whose life was as disordered and sad as his art was delicate, moving and influential. He destroyed his marriage by his liaison with the young poet Arthur Rimbaud, an affair that ended with his shooting Rimbaud and serving two years in prison.

His life after his release did not much improve: he slid back into alcoholism and debauchery; but he went on making poems, some of them very touching.

Octaves, XI Triangulation, in astronomy, is a way of measuring the distance of stars by geometrical calculation, but it is useful only for stars that are no more than a few thousand light-years away. *Untriangulated stars* are the very distant ones. (*Untriangulated Stars* is the title Denham Sutcliffe gave to his edition of Robinson's letters to Harry DeForest Smith.)

Isaac and Archibald A *hackmatack* is a balsam poplar. An *astrakhan* is here a variety of apple. *John Flaxman,* 1755–1826, was a sculptor and draftsman who made drawings of figures on Greek vases to illustrate volumes of Homer, Æschylus, and others. (Some of the drawings were engraved by his friend, the poet William Blake.)

Aunt Imogen Aunt Imogen is, at least partly, a figure for Robinson himself, whose only family after the deaths of his parents and brothers was that of his sister-in-law and three nieces, whom he adored and in whose childish play he took part. *Harlequin* is a stock figure from the commedia dell'arte, a prankster who continually discomfits and deflates the clown. In his later incarnation in English pantomime, he is generally mischievous, as well as invisible to all eyes but those of his beloved Columbine; she too is sometimes invisible to mortals.

Erasmus Desiderius Erasmus, 1466?–1536, Dutch scholar, priest and theologian, who produced editions of classical authors and wrote a number of important books, the best known of which is *In Praise of Folly*. Hoping to restore simple faith based on Scripture and to instigate reforms in the Church of Rome, he also criticized Luther and the doctrine of predestination.

Cortège Very little can be made of this ditty without knowing at least some of the biographical facts (or, one might say, the biographical legend). Robinson's brother Herman and his brother's bride, Emma, with whom Robinson was hopelessly in love, departed on their honeymoon on the four o'clock train to St. Louis, roughly fifteen hundred miles from Gardiner, Maine. The talk of a *grave for them* is startling; we can only guess at the intensity of this gentle young man's feelings of betrayal and abandonment.

Variations of Greek Themes   Although Robinson modestly hesitates to call these poems translations, it is hard to know what else to call them. At the time Robinson was doing them, he wrote to a friend: "In making the translations—if they may be called translations—I used Mackail's *Selections,* and used them most shamelessly—I mean the English part of them—for my knowledge of Greek was never more than Xenophontic, and now it isn't even that." He does permit himself a number of liberties, but no more than many translators. Here are the prose versions from J. W. Mackail's book, *Select Epigrams from the Greek Anthology* (with Mackail's titles), the versions that Robinson worked from; the reader can judge for himself.

"A Happy Man" by Carphyllides:
EARTH'S FELICITY
Find no fault as thou passest by my monument, O wayfarer; not even in death have I aught worthy of lamentation. I have left children's children; I had joy of one wife, who grew old along with me; I made marriage for three sons whose sons I often lulled asleep on my breast, and never moaned over the sickness or death of any: who, shedding tears without sorrow over me, sent me to slumber the sweet sleep in the country of the holy.

"A Mighty Runner" by Nicarchus:
SLOW AND SURE
Charmus ran for the three miles in Arcadia with five others; surprising to say, he actually came in seventh. When there were only six, perhaps you will say, how seventh? A friend of his went along in his great-coat, crying, "Keep it up, Charmus!" and so he arrives seventh; and if only he had had five more friends, Zoilus, he would have come in twelfth.

"The Raven" by Nicarchus:

THE POPULAR SINGER

The night-raven's song is deadly; but when Demophilus sings, even the night-raven dies.

"Eutychides" by Lucilius:

POPULAR SONGS

Eutychides, the writer of songs, is dead; flee, O you under earth! Eutychides is coming with his odes; he left instructions to burn along with him twelve lyres and twenty-five boxes of airs. Now the bitterness of death has come upon you; whither may one retreat in future, since Eutychides fills Hades too?

(Mackail is not quite literal here, giving the abstract phrase, "the bitterness of death," where the Greek has *Charon*—the ferryman who rows the newly dead across the Styx.) Eutychides is one of Lucilius' favorite laughingstocks; he may well be the son of Eutychus, whom Lucilius made sport of in this witty epigram, nailing Eutychides at the same time:

Eutychus the portrait-painter got twenty sons, and never got one likeness, even among his children.

"Doricha" by Posidippus:

SAPPHO

Doricha, long ago thy bones are dust, and the ribbons of thy hair and the raiment scented with unguents, wherein once wrapping lovely Charaxus round thou didst cling to him, carousing into dawn; but the white leaves of the dear ode of Sappho remain yet and shall remain speaking thine adorable name, which Naucratis shall keep here so long as a sea-going ship shall come to the lagoons of Nile.

Charaxus was the brother of Sappho, the great lyric poet of Lesbos. *Naucratis,* an ancient Egyptian city on the Nile, south of Alexandria, was the first Greek colony in Egypt, seventh century BCE, and, according to Mackail's note, the only open port in Egypt before the Persian conquest.

"The Dust of Timas" by Sappho is the only poem in this sequence which is not from Mackail's anthology; the following version is from the *Greek Lyric* volume of *Loeb's Classical Library:*

This is the dust of Timas. She died before her marriage and was received by the dark chamber of Persephone. On her death all her companions took the lovely hair from their heads with newly sharpened steel.

Back to Mackail.

"Aretemias" by Antipater of Sidon:
SUNDERING
Surely, methinks, when thou hadst set thy footprint, Aretemias, from the boat upon Cocytus' shore, carrying in thy young hand thy baby just dead, the fair Dorian women had compassion in Hades, inquiring of thy fate; and thou, fretting thy cheeks with tears, didst utter that woeful word: "O friends, having travailed of two children, I left one for my husband Euphron, and the other I bring to the dead."

Cocytus, like the Styx, is one of the five rivers of Hades.

"The Old Story" by Marcus Argentarius:
LIGHT LOVE
Thou wert loved when rich, Sosicrates, but being poor thou art loved no longer; what magic has hunger! and she who before called thee spice and darling Adonis, Menophila, now inquires thy name. Who and whence of men art thou? where is thy city? Surely thou art dull in learning this saying, that none is friend to him who has nothing.

"Tomorrow" by Macedonius the Consul:

"Tomorrow I will look on thee"—but that never comes for us, while the accustomed putting-off ever grows and grows. This is all thy kindness to my longing; but to others thou bearest other gifts, despising my faithful service. "I will see thee at evening."

But what is the evening of a woman's life? old age full of a million wrinkles.

"Laïs to Aphroditê" is ascribed to Plato in the *Palatine Anthology*, but although it sometimes still bears his name, scholars say it must have been written much later:

TO APHRODITÊ, BY LAÏS

I Laïs who laughed exultant over Greece, I who held that swarm of young lovers in my porches, lay my mirror before the Paphian; since such as I am I will not see myself, and such as I was I cannot.

There were two famous courtesans named Laïs, separated by nearly a century. The *Paphian* is Aphroditê, so called because the city of Paphos on Cyprus was sacred to her worship. For whatever interest it may have, here is Dudley Fitts' version, closer and prosier than Robinson's, and my own, which takes even more liberties than his does:

I Laïs whose laughter was scornful in Hellas,
Whose doorways were thronged daily with young lovers,
I dedicate my mirror to Aphroditê:

For I will not see myself as I am now,
And cannot see myself as once I was.

LAÏS DEDICATES TO APHRODITÊ THE TOOLS
   OF HER TRADE

Words cannot say what she was in her prime,
This Laïs, now a specimen of Time.
She used to laugh to see so many men,
Not one of whom she'll ever see again.

Goddess, to you I yield my useless mirror—
What can it do but verify Time's error?
It will not show me as I used to be,
And what it will show I refuse to see.

"An Inscription by the Sea" by Glaucus:
ON THE EMPTY TOMB OF ONE LOST AT SEA
Not dust nor the light weight of a stone, but all this sea that
thou beholdest is the tomb of Erasippus; for he perished with
his ship, and in some unknown place his bones moulder, and the
seagulls alone know them to tell.

Momus Momus is an eponym for someone who is constantly
complaining and mocking. Momus, the son of Night, was the
god of ridicule and carping. Even the other gods could not
live up to his standards: he opined that Aphroditê did not walk
quietly enough, that Zeus should have put the bull's horns on
its shoulders. Eventually, fed up with his constant criticism,
the gods banished him. *King Kronos,* or Kronus (identified by
the Romans with Saturn), was one of the Titans; he overthrew
his father and was overthrown in turn by his son, Zeus. John
Hollander has pointed out to me that the question Momus
asks in the second stanza, *What's become of / Browning?* echoes
Browning's own poem, "Waring," which begins,

> What's become of Waring
> Since he gave us all the slip. . . .

The White Lights This poem was written to celebrate the great
success of William Vaughn Moody's play, *The Great Divide.*
Moody was a long-time friend and rival—a poet of some
fame in his day, but now almost completely forgotten. *Flaccus*
is the cognomen of Horace (see "Horace to Leuconoë") and
Maro that of Virgil (*the Mantuan,* i.e., the man from Mantua),
whom Robinson praises by calling his language *alembic*—an
alembic is a kind of still for purifying liquids; as far as I can
tell, this was the first time that the word had been used as an
adjective. *Avalon,* in Celtic mythology, is the Island of Blessed
Souls, where King Arthur was buried and from which he was
to return. It is difficult to say just what Robinson means,
since Shakespeare made no use of Arthurian legend—per-

haps he has in mind a continuity of poetic spirit on English soil.

How Annandale Went Out   Annandale is a character who appears in other poems, notably the longish poem "The Book of Annandale." The speaker has apparently helped him to die; the *slight sort of engine* is probably a hypodermic. (For anyone familiar with Robinson's life, this poem cannot but call to mind the death of his brother Dean, a doctor, who died of an overdose of morphine, self-administered and almost certainly deliberate.)

For a Dead Lady   The lady is Mary Palmer Robinson, the poet's mother, who died in 1896, only days before his first book, *The Torrent and the Night Before*, was published.

The Revealer   Robinson is generally not at his best when he deals with a political subject head-on, and this poem, although better than his tribute to Lincoln, is not without flaws. But I felt that it ought to be included because of Robinson's debt to Theodore Roosevelt, whose remarkable response to *The Children of the Night* meant so much to him, bringing him his first widespread recognition and a sinecure to rescue him from poverty. Although egalitarian and sympathetic in his personal relations, Robinson almost always expresses, as here, a mistrust of popular rule and a conviction that a workable democracy depends on the rule of superior men. *A Tyrian heritage* is a figurative way of speaking of America's pride in its wealth and power—Tyre was the center of Phœnician commerce. The *lions* perhaps represent the great trusts and monopolies that Roosevelt worked to break up. It is hard to say what the *small cloud* might be—possibly an allusion to the "little cloud out of the sea, like a man's hand," the harbinger of the great rain so long awaited (I Kings 18: 44)? The *combs* must be the ill-gotten gains of the plutocrats. There is a very considerable difference between a *Nazarite* and a *Nazarene*—a Nazarite (from a root meaning "separate") is one who takes a vow to abstain from wine, to keep his distance from dead bodies, and to let his hair and beard grow, never to be cut; Samson was a Nazarite (although he took only the last of the three vows). A Nazarene is a native of Nazareth, and the name came to mean Jesus or his disciples. *An Angel with a Sword* refers to the "Cherubims [sic] and a flaming sword which turned every way, to keep the way of the tree of life" and keep Adam and Eve out. But identifying these allusions can help only so far— "The Revealer" remains a somewhat obscure poem.

The Gift of God After Robinson's death, Emma Robinson and her daughter Ruth put together a commentary on his poems (of which Danny Smith has kindly sent me a copy). Of this poem Emma said, "H.E.R. [Herman]. He was perfectly satisfactory to his parents and idolized by them."

John Gorham This poem is written in a folk meter, dipodic, which is employed in many nursery rhymes and ballads. A dipod, or dipody, is a double foot with one strong accent and one secondary one; the number of syllables can vary considerably. For example:

Try to **LOOK** as ɪF the **MOON** were ᴍᴀᴋing **FAC**ᴇs **AT** you,
And a **LIT**tle **MORE** as **IF** you **MEANT** to **STAY** a **LIT**tle
WHILE.

It is also the meter of "Leonora" and "The Valley of the Shadow."

Hillcrest The name of Mrs. Edward MacDowell's farmhouse. The widow of the famous composer founded a writer's colony in New Hampshire, where Robinson stayed every summer from 1911 until 1934, the year before he died.

Ben Jonson Entertains a Man from Stratford *Terpander* was a Greek poet from Lesbos, regarded as the founder of Greek classical music and lyric poetry. (He either increased the number of strings of the lyre from four to seven, or increased the divisions of the ode from four to seven—scholars dispute which.) *Naiads* are the nymphs of wells and springs, etc. *The unities* are one of Aristotle's curious theories, according to which a play should consist of one main action that takes place in one day and in one place. (There are very few plays, Greek or otherwise, that obey this "rule.") *Greene* is the dramatist who wrote the famous sneer at Shakespeare, calling him "an upstart crow beautified with our feathers." *The Globe* was the theatre of Shakespeare's company, the Lord Chamberlain's Players (later the King's Men). *Tophet* is the underworld where wicked souls suffer torments. *The Cyprian,* like the Paphian, is Aphroditê. *Katharsis* is Aristotle's term for the effect of tragic drama, which cleanses us first by evoking and then by purging us of pity and fear. Ben Jonson was a better scholar than his friend and is said to have instructed him in Aristotle's poetics, or tried to. As Aubrey tells us in his *Brief Lives,* Jonson said of Shakespeare "that he had but little Latin and less Greek."

Eros Turannos The title means Love, the Tyrant. Some of the words we encounter seem slightly surprising, however plain and simple—like *engaging,* which contains a thrilling dissonance of several different meanings. Here we suddenly have a sense of the man's charm, his pledges and commitments, his persuasions, and behind all of this, shadowy notions of ensnarements and interlockings—even battle. *All* reasons are overcome by another fear, that of growing old *alone.* Why is it that being *drawn slowly* toward the end seems somehow more frightening? Or, for me, yet more mysterious and full of dread, *foamless.* The meter is so strict and regular that when we come to *Vibrate,* the first trochaic substitution in 32 lines, it registers with a force that trochees rarely have (and perhaps because of this, I experience, beyond the metaphorical sense of the townspeople's gossipy buzz, an image almost hallucinatory: the literal meaning). Donald Justice has written a luminous and memorable account of this great poem in his essay, "Benign Obscurity"; the following sentences are excerpted from some four pages of commentary: "There are things about this poem we will never know, just as there are things about it we seem to have known even before we started reading it. For one of its secrets is that it is based on a classic story situation, one we may think we understand better than in fact we do simply because we recognize it. . . . Such compression as it has comes about because the prose details are, practically speaking, left out; they have been transformed into generality, an abstract or summary; the language, instead of being heated-up and rich, seems barely adequate to contain the force of the bottled-up emotion of the poem, which keeps threatening to break out. . . . It is the dramatic situation here that seems to add a suggestiveness and depth to the unspectacular words of the poem. It is as if we caught glimpses of a moral complexity through the chinks in the logic of its expression. If this is so, we can at least suggest that some of the obscurity is expressive of the very understanding the poem is intended to carry. . . . The truth, whatever it may be, is held in suspension, unresolved: that itself is the resolution, the final truth. If the poem seems in the end somehow more definite than this as you look back upon it, put it down to the eloquence of the last stanza and especially of the last four or five lines, which are bound to ring and echo in the memory as if no more could possibly have been said."

Old Trails *Boris* is the Moussorgsky opera, *Boris Godunov,* based on one of Pushkin's plays. (Godunov was a favorite of Ivan the Terrible; after Ivan's death in 1584, Godunov had his heir Dmitri murdered, wielded power as the regent of the other son, and ascended to the throne in 1598.) The narrator has complicated feelings about this failed friend come back to his old haunts in Greenwich Village, resolved to put the past behind him, take leave of the ghosts, and make a new start. The narrator, however skeptical of his friend's motives and talents, is too generous not to be happy for his triumph when it finally comes, after the five years of toil (in Yonkers of all places!), but there is more than one suggestion that the success is not altogether real or worthy. There is an "evil and infirm perversity" in the man and he must acknowledge the reproach implicit in his companion's silence. He has responded to Broadway's siren-calls; he will take the safer way by giving the crowd what it wants and leave this down-at-heel little Bohemia behind forever. He is not a vicious man, like the protagonist of the opera they attend after dinner, but his success might be regarded as similarly callous and tainted. (Robinson, like the narrator, chose "growing old alone among the ghosts." He did make one failed attempt at the stage not very long before this poem was written; his two plays, *The Porcupine* and *Van Zorn*, were never produced.)

The Unforgiven   Emma's glosses on the poems, although sometimes clearly mistaken, are interesting and worth considering. Her response to "Eros Turannos": "Despotic love. E.L.R. [Emma] and H.E.R. [Herman]: their downfall." Of this poem she says, "Once more, the wreckage of their marriage. His point of view as opposed to hers in 'Eros Turannos.' " I have my doubts about her reading of that poem; here I think she is on the mark.

Veteran Sirens   *Ninon* is Anne de Lenclos (Ninon is a nickname for Anne), 1615–1705, a famous beauty and wit whose salon was one of the most fashionable in Paris. She had many distinguished lovers, including La Rochefoucauld, and in her old age she was a generous friend to the young Voltaire. *Time's malicious mercy* is a trenchant oxymoron; I would guess that number and space, which the old prostitutes have been cautioned to think of, have to do with the impersonal reality of the fleeting years, and the dangers, degradations and extremities that the women are hemmed in by. In the first decade or so of this century, whores were still to some extent a shocking subject—at least in poetry.

Bokardo   Robinson said that in a course in logic he took while at Harvard, his professor, George Herbert Palmer, "said the Bokardo was a figure which no one understood, and I took it

as a symbol of the mystery of things." It is the name of a log-
ical syllogism—"an exceptional case, which must be proven
indirectly by reductio ad absurdum": some B are not C; all B
are A; therefore, some A are not C. (The Bocardo was also a
prison in the old north gate of Oxford, named after the syllo-
gism. Stephen Young tells me that it is referred to in a play by
Robert Greene, *Friar Bacon and Friar Bungay.* At one point, an
Oxford doctor, fed up with the witty mockery of a poor scholar,
cries, "Call out the beadles and convey them hence, / Straight
to Bocardo; let the roisters lie / Close clapped in bolts, until
their wits be tame.") The strange drama of this poem may be
clarified somewhat in light of what little we know about the
relationship between Robinson and his brother—we may re-
gard the speaker as standing for Robinson, who is addressing
his brother Herman. Although for the most part he was gen-
erous and forgiving toward his brother, he may have had rea-
son to suspect him of cheating him out of part of his
patrimony, and he must have felt great anger that Herman had
married the woman he regarded as his soul mate. *Xerxes* was
the king of Persia, 510–465 BCE—he built a pontoon bridge
across the Hellespont during his invasion of Greece and was
so enraged when it was swept away by the breakers that he in-
flicted 300 lashes on the disobedient sea and cast chains of
iron across it. The irony is typically Robinsonian in its tone
and its style of wit.

The Valley of the Shadow   This remarkable poem, for all its
Dantesque vision of some circle of hell, is not, I think, about
the afterlife; it might well have been called *The Valley of the
Shadow of Life.* A line that Alan Trachtenberg picked out
for particular praise is one that I too find praiseworthy, and in-
teresting for its clear echo of Hardy: "At a measureless
malfeasance that obscurely willed it thus." (Robinson loved
Hardy's poetry, but this is one of the very few places where he
sounds like him.) John Hollander says that "Robinson gener-
ates a new fiction out of [the biblical phrase]" and points out

other voices besides Hardy, such as Shelley, Swinburne, and Nietzsche.

The Wandering Jew This is one of Robinson's four or five greatest poems; it is, like much of his verse, very sparing in its images, employing a diction almost entirely abstract. *Nathan* was the prophet to whom the Lord came in a vision, commanding him to bless David and prophesy the coming greatness of Israel; who was later sent to accuse him of having lain with Bathsheba and plotting her husband Uriah's death. *Lamech*, descended from Cain, lived 777 years and fathered Noah (Genesis 4: 18 and 5: 25–30); *Abimelech* was the King of Gerar, to whom Abraham in fear for his life gave Sarah, saying that she was his sister, and to whom God came in a dream to say that Sarah was the prophet's wife and not to be touched (Genesis, 20); *Melchizedek* was a high priest, probably of a Canaanite cult (Genesis 14: 18–20). *The Wandering Jew*, according to the medieval legend, is a cobbler named Ahasuerus (sometimes identified as Cartaphilus, Pilate's doorkeeper), who strikes Jesus on his way to Calvary, refuses to let him rest, and shouts at him to go faster. Jesus replies, "Truly I go away, and that quickly, but thou shalt tarry till I come again"—the man is condemned to lose the power to die and must go on living until the Second Coming. He stands in particular contrast to Melchizedek, who recognized Abraham as God's chosen and blessed him.

The Three Taverns *Herodion* is Paul's kinsman; *Apelles* and *Amplias* are friends and disciples (Romans 16: 8–10). *Andronicus* had formerly been in prison with Paul (Romans 16: 7). *Cæsarea* was a seaport built by Herod the Great that later became the capital of Roman Palestine, and Paul was imprisoned there for two years or more, after the Sadducees had denounced him to the Romans (and plotted to kill him) for his belief in the resurrection of the dead. *Festus* was the Procurator of Judæa; *Agrippa* (Marcus Julius Agrippa II) was king. Paul had refused to go to Jerusalem to be tried; he was a Roman citizen and as such insisted on being tried in Rome. After his eloquent speech in his own defense, Agrippa said quietly to Festus, "This man doeth nothing worthy of death or of bonds. [He] might have been set at liberty, if he had not appealed unto Cæsar." The long voyage to Rome in mid-winter was slowed by severe weather; after the shipwreck of a second vessel and several months' delay, the centurions and their prisoners finally embarked from Alexandria and slowly made their way to Rome: ". . . . when the brethren heard of us, they came to meet us as far as Appii forum, and The three taverns." The forum was 43 miles from Rome, the Three Taverns 33 miles, along the Appian Way. It is a gripping story and can be found in Acts 21–28. *Stephen* is St. Stephen, the first Christian martyr; sometime before Paul's conversion, he was falsely charged with blasphemy and insurrection and stoned to death; Paul (then Saul, and a righteous persecutor of Christians) had consented to the sentence, and he was present when it was carried out (Acts 6–8)—the stone-throwers cast off some of their clothes for the hot work, dropping them near his feet. (Anthony Hecht has written a brilliant and frightening poem about an analogous scene, called "The Feast of Stephen.") *Gamaliel* (Rabban Gamaliel) had spoken in defense of Stephen and the other apostles, counseling the angry Jews to spare their lives. (*His* father had been the young Saul's teacher.) There are several allusions throughout the monologue to Paul's various epistles.

The Flying Dutchman   According to one version of the legend, a Dutch sea captain insists on rounding the Cape of Good Hope in spite of a violent storm and the terror of everyone else on board. The figure of God Himself appears, but the captain fires on it and utters terrible blasphemies. For this he is condemned to sail on forever without finding harbor, and his ghostly ship to lure other vessels to their destruction. I see the captain as an exemplar of Emersonian self-reliance with a

vengeance—self-reliance gone berserk—and I read the poem
as a little allegory that dramatizes the poet's unblinkered vi-
sion of the individual will in isolation from the community
and its perhaps fated damnation; it may also be a judgment of
the modern sciences—in short, of all human suffering that
appears to arise from blind ambition and hubris. Emma, as
usual, found the family drama at the heart of the poem:
"H.E.R. again: his self-sufficiency and ruin."

John Brown   Robinson seems to have drawn on several of the let-
ters that Brown wrote during November of 1859 as he awaited
execution for his seizure and occupation of the Federal arse-
nal at Harper's Ferry, but his principal source was Brown's last
letter to his family, dated November 30th and addressed to
"My Dearly beloved Wife, Sons: & Daughters, *every one*." All
of the essential themes of the poem are expressed there:
Brown's view of his death, his role as prophet, his usefulness
as a dead man and martyr to the cause, his justifications for
what he has done. John Stauffer, who kindly sent me the let-
ters and who knows this material intimately, observes that
Robinson's verse has captured Brown's language and cadences
with wonderful fidelity, and I agree.

Souvenir   The word is French here and means *remembrance, recol-
lection.*

Firelight   Although distinctively Robinsonian in character, the
irony of this little drama may owe something to Hardy's
Satires of Circumstance, which Robinson would certainly have
read.

Late Summer   Another poem that can be better understood if we
read it as dramatizing the poet's passionate lifelong love for
his sister-in-law, her own inner conflicts, and her refusal fi-
nally to yield to his importunities. The poem was published in
1920; Herman was now dead ("and would come again /
Never"); and Robinson had been in love with Emma for thirty

years. Chard Powers Smith believes, I think reasonably, that she knew from the very beginning what Robinson began to realize only a few years before his death, that he did not really want to marry anyone. *Alcaics* is a meter named for the poet Alkaios. It is usually a quatrain, and the scheme can easily be worked out by reading the lines aloud—and counting. (In English, quantitative meter is extremely difficult and rarely successful, and most poets have converted it to our own measures, attending to syllables and accents instead of quantities.) Lines 1 and 2 have eleven syllables, line 3 has nine, and line 4 has ten. Robinson here makes pentameters out of the two hendecasyllabic lines and four-beaters out of the two shorter lines, and also keeps the exact syllable count. Horace loved this form and used it many times, and English poets have also experimented with it, most notably Tennyson. I think that the most exquisite example, especially in its cadences, is Auden's great elegy, "In Memory of Sigmund Freud"; here is the last stanza:

> One rational voice is dumb. Over his grave
> the household of Impulse mourns one dearly loved:
>   sad is Eros, builder of cities,
>   and weeping anarchic Aphrodite.

Mr. Flood's Party   "*The bird is on the wing*"—that Mr. Flood had read Edward Fitzgerald's beautiful translation of *The Rubáiyát of Omar Khayyám* when he was younger suggests that there is more to him than alcoholism and loneliness. The reference is to stanza VII:

> Come, fill the Cup, and in the fire of Spring
> Your Winter-garment of Repentance fling:
>   The Bird of Time has but a little way
>   To flutter—and the Bird is on the Wing.

Roland's ghost is a brilliant simile, its irony encompassing both gentle mockery and heartfelt admiration. Roland was one of Charlemagne's captains, commanding the rear guard during the return of the Frankish army from its invasion of Spain in 778 BCE, when his detachment was attacked at Roncesvalles, a pass in the Pyrenees, by a pursuing force of Navarrese or Basques. Brave to a fault and too proud to summon help, Roland turns to engage the enemy, who greatly outnumber his men. When at last he does blow his horn, it is too late—the rear guard is slaughtered to the last man. The physical comparison between the soldier blowing his horn and the solitary drunk lifting his jug to his lips is funny and touching, but they also resemble each other, the young captain and the old rummy, in their forlorn pride and courage, and in their nearness to death. (Roland's valor became the stuff of legend and epic poetry, flowering several centuries later in the *Chanson de Roland* and then again in Ariosto's epic, *Orlando Furioso*.) Frost has written a lovely passage about the tender irony of *only two moons listening:* "The guarded pathos of 'Mr. Flood's Party' is what makes it merciless. We are to bear in mind the number of moons listening. Two, as on the planet Mars. No less. No more ('No more, sir, that's enough'). One moon (albeit a moon, no sun) would have laid grief too bare. More than two would have dissipated grief entirely and would have amounted to dissipation. The emotion had to be held at a point." (That is good enough that we must forgive the misquotation.)

Ben Trovato   Another rather Hardyesque little poem, relishing the grotesque. There is considerably more of this ironic humor, of wit and humor in general, in Robinson than readers have been led to expect. Even the title is a kind of joke, Mr. Trovato's name having been taken from the old Italian saw, "Si non è vero, è ben trovato"—*If it isn't true, it ought to be.* (I am indebted, once again, to John Hollander for this information.) Emma's perceptive comment: "The strategem—as of Jacob's blessing."

The Tree in Pamela's Garden   The tree, which does not appear in the poem, must represent the tree of the knowledge of good and evil; presumably Pamela, unlike Eve, has not eaten of its fruit. It has been suggested that she may have a secret lover, but that seems unlikely. She is too gentle to deceive her roses, or anyone else for that matter, and her solicitous neighbors may pity her to their hearts' content.

Lost Anchors   This compelling sonnet is rather oblique in its bits and hints of narrative—too indirect, surely, to be read on the run. We are not told the legend of the ship or even part of it, either before or after its sinking; all we know is that it has lain at the bottom of the harbor for a century or more, and that divers had found its anchors and seized them (*seized* meaning perhaps, both stolen them and, in its nautical sense, tied them together). *Misadventure* is a puzzle. I take it that the appropriation of the anchors is analogous to the old man's life in that he too has lost his anchors, so to speak; he is useless and out of his element, warped by age, or by his own misadventures, and embittered enough to wish that he had never been born.

Afterthoughts   What the man comes back to say is brief and, by the standards of the worldly and ambitious, insignificant, but the speaker is impressed by its import, perhaps by its revelation of unsuspected spiritual qualities. The *Delphic heights* were above the Oracle and the temple sacred to Apollo, so this man has not climbed Parnassus, he is not a poet.

Caput Mortuum   Literally, "death's head," what alchemists called the residue remaining in a flask after distillation; it is now taken to mean any worthless residue, or even a worthless person—a poet, for instance, living in a world that values money and status and depreciates art. We can take the ghostly visitor as a stand-in for Robinson himself.

Monadnock Through the Trees   Monadnock is an isolated peak in southern New Hampshire. Robinson had a good view of it from his cabin at the MacDowell Colony, and a much better one after some intervening trees were cut down (as in *Archibald's Example*). Robinson certainly knew and may have had in mind Emerson's long poem, *Monadnoc*, as well as Hardy's sonnet *Zermatt: To the Matterhorn*.

Many Are Called   Matthew 22: 14: "For many are called, but few are chosen." *Apollo* is one of the most important Olympian gods, both for the Greeks and the Romans, sometimes called Phœbus, the god of light, and later identified with Helios, the sun god. He is the god of poetry and music (not to mention medicine, archery, prophecy and so on).

Rembrandt to Rembrandt   The oddness of the date given to this monologue may reflect the influence on Robinson of the legend then current of the great painter scorned by his bourgeois countrymen for his honesty and unflinching realism. In 1645, Rembrandt has many pupils and major commissions and use of the considerable funds that were his late wife's dowry—he is buying, and will go on buying for several more years, expensive paintings and engravings for his large collection. *Franz* (Frans Hals) *is* popular and successful, but, ironically, he will be declared bankrupt only seven years after the date of this monologue, four years before Rembrandt's own bankruptcy in 1656 (a disaster caused largely by his own financial mismanagement, and not really by the incomprehension and dissatisfaction of his public). Hals was a marvelous and original painter, not the cynical panderer to bourgeois taste he is here made out to be. But in spite of the biographical inaccuracies, this is an impressive study of the isolated artist. It very likely has more to do with Robinson and the decades of poverty and neglect that *he* endured than with the painter's actual career. *Saskia* is Rembrandt's late wife, whom he loved, and whom he painted again and again. *Titus* is his son, the only one of Saskia's four children to survive. *Mynheer* is a term of formal address, which is still in constant use in Holland. It might occasionally be spoken these days with a touch of class-

Notes to pages 185—188 · 239

conscious irony. The painter's greeting to his self-portrait would be best rendered by something like, "Rembrandt, my dear sir." (If he is being ironic, it is a slightly different irony.)

A Man in Our Town   Emma saw this sonnet as "a beautiful tribute to his brother Dean. Even after he was so completely subjected to the fetters of opium that he no longer practiced his profession, or operated his drug store, he was called back to the Savings Bank to help balance their accounts, and called to the medical emergencies of neighbors."

New England   Passion, Love, Joy, and Conscience seem to be the dreariest of allegorical emblems, but we should not overlook the quietly ironic but decisive clause, "We're told." Robinson was nonplussed and annoyed to hear that readers had taken this poem as an attack on New England and Puritan values. It is nothing of the kind. In response to the imbroglio stirred up by the poem, Robinson wrote a letter to the daily newspaper in Gardiner, saying, "I cannot quite see how the first eight lines of my sonnet are to be regarded as even intelligible if read in any other way than as an oblique attack upon all those who are forever throwing dead cats at New England for its alleged emotional and moral frigidity. As for the last six lines, I should suppose that the deliberate insertion of 'It seems' would be enough to indicate the key in which they are written."

Reunion   This sonnet is very likely about a meeting with Emma in the late twenties when she made clear to him in no uncertain terms that she was not willing to marry him.

INDEX OF TITLES AND FIRST LINES

A NOTE ON THE TYPE

The principal text of this Modern Library edition
was set in a digitized version of Janson,
a typeface that dates from about 1690 and was cut by Nicholas Kis,
a Hungarian working in Amsterdam. The original matrices have
survived and are held by the Stempel foundry in Germany.
Hermann Zapf redesigned some of the weights and sizes for Stempel,
basing his revisions on the original design.